Meredith Hooper
Entering the Ark
Hunting in the Marshes
January

D1823689

SUPPORT MATERIALS

TEACHER'S BOOK 1: Beginning to Read

Listening Pictures (Phonics Flipover Book)

Sounds Fun! (Phonic Games Pack)

BIG BOOKS
The Cambridge Big Book of Nursery Rhymes
Walking in the Jungle/A Very Hot Day
I Went to School This Morning/What For?

SIGHT VOCABULARY WORKBOOKS
The First Fifty Words: Books 1 to 3

COMPUTER SOFTWARE

CASSETTE

INFORMATION BOOKS

Meredith Hooper
Dinosaur*
Osprey
Seal

The Bridge
The Forest
The Harbour

Phil Gates
Animal Senses
Bubbles*
The Scots Pine

SUPPORT MATERIALS

TEACHER'S BOOK 2: Becoming a Reader

Sounds Fun! (Phonic Games Pack)

THE INFORMATION BOOKS TEACHER'S GUIDE 1: Becoming a Reader

BIG BOOKS
Bubbles
Dinosaur
Wayne's Box
What's the Time?

SIGHT VOCABULARY WORKBOOKS
The First Fifty Words: Books 4 and 5

COMPUTER SOFTWARE

CASSETTE

Phil Gates
Animal Communication
Camouflage*
Codes and Signals

Meredith Hooper
A Book of Hours
Noah's Ark
The Tomb of Nebamun

Coral Reef*
Desert
Rainforest

SUPPORT MATERIALS

TEACHER'S BOOK 3: Towards Independence

THE INFORMATION BOOKS TEACHER'S GUIDE 2: Towards Independence

Phonics into Spelling (Teacher's Resource)

BIG BOOKS
Camouflage
Coral Reef

COMPUTER SOFTWARE

CASSETTES

Richard Brown/Kate Ruttle	Kate Ruttle/Richard Brown	Rosemary Davidson
Jumping	*Hey Diddle Diddle*	*Fishy Numbers*
Looking for Dragons	*Hickory, Dickory, Dock*	
*Walking in the Jungle**	*Humpty Dumpty*	
	Incy Wincy Spider	

Afloat in a Boat		*One Teddy All Alone*
*I Went to School This Morning**		

TRADITIONAL	STORIES OF CHILDHOOD	POETRY AND RHYME
Gerald Rose	**Juliet Partridge**	**Kate Ruttle/Richard Brown**
The Gingerbread Man	*Going Fishing*	*Five Little Monkeys*
The Lion and the Mouse	**Sue Perry/Jane Rose**	*One Blue Hen*
The Raven and the Fox	*Not Yet, Nathan!*	*Two by Two*
	Gerald Rose	
	Bad Boy, Billy!	
The Clever Tortoise	**Richard Brown**	*Over in the Meadow*
The Little Red Hen	*All by Myself*	*Peas in a Pod*
The Tortoise and the Hare	*The Moonlit Owl*	*Wiggle and Giggle*
	Grace Hallworth/Richard Brown	
	Going to School	
Joanna Troughton	*Gracie's Cat*	**Marjorie Craggs**
The Animal Wrestlers	**Richard Brown**	*Rhyming Riddles*
The Chinese New Year	*Atul's Christmas Hamster*	**Grace Hallworth**
The Story of Running Water	**Gerald Rose**	*Sleep Tight*
	Tiger Dreams	**Juliet Partridge**
		Everyone is Reading

Mona Green/Pamela Lofts	**Richard Brown**	**Richard Brown/Kate Ruttle**
How the Animals Got Their Tails	*Ben's Amazing Birthday*	*In the Mirror*
Grace Hallworth	*Dad's Promise*	*Marvel Paws*
Dancing to the River	*Tulips for Dad*	*Nonsense!*
Duncan Williamson/Linda Williamson		
Rabbit's Tail		
Rosalind Kerven	*A Welsh Lamb*	*A Corner of Magic*
The Weather Drum	*Dancing in Soot*	*A Lick of the Spoon*
Volcano Woman	*The Haystack*	*Knickerbocker Number Nine*
Keith Ruttle		
The Lord Mount Dragon		
Antonia Barber	*A Shoot of Corn*	*A Mosquito in the Cabin*
The Cape of Rushes	*Snow in the Kitchen*	*Out and About*
Debjani Chatterjee	*The Watch by the Sea*	*Welcome Night*
The Most Beautiful Child		
Rosalind Kerven		
Coyote Girl		

Cambridge Reading

BEGINNING TO READ
MAINLY RECEPTION/PRIMARY 1

A

Bill Gillham
Two Babies
What's in the Box?

Juliet Partridge
A Very Hot Day*
The Picnic

B

Dirty Dog
My Dog's Party
My Pet
Guess Who I Am!
What For?*
Where's Woolly?

Blowing Bubbles
That's Me!
Five Green Monsters
Four Scary Monsters
Three Spotty Monsters
All Fall Down!

*Also in Big Book format

BECOMING A READER
MAINLY YEAR 1/PRIMARY 2

	CONTEMPORARY	FANTASY
A	**Tony Bradman** *Here Comes Everyone* *This is the Register* *What's the TIme?**	**John Prater** *Dan's Box* *Lucy's Box* *Wayne's Box**
B	*Follow My Leader* *Please, Miss!* *Show-and-Tell*	*Billy's Box* *Sophie's Box* *Yasmin's Box*
C	*A Friend for Kate* *Imran and the Watch* *Well Done, Sam!*	*Nishal's Box* *Tom's Box* *Vicky's Box*

*Also in Big Book format

TOWARDS INDEPENDENCE
MAINLY YEAR 2/PRIMARY 3

A	**June Crebbin** *Cutting and Sticking* *Parrot Talk* *Strawberry Picking*	**Rosemary Hayes** *The Big Shrink* *The Grabbing Bird* *The Treasure Cave*
B	*The Dog Show* *The Pyjama Party* *The Special Cake*	*Jumble Power* *The Magic Sword* *The Peace Ring*
C	*A Cat for Keeps* *Don't Be Late!* *Spike and the Concert*	*Mr Mulch's Magic Mixtures* *The Amazing Mr Mulch* *The Slippery Planet*

*Also in Big Book format

Towards Independence

Richard Brown
and Kate Ruttle

General Editors

Richard Brown
and Kate Ruttle

Consultant Editor

Jean Glasberg

PUBLISHED BY THE PRESS SYNDICATE OF THE UNIVERSITY OF CAMBRIDGE
The Pitt Building, Trumpington Street, Cambridge CB2 1RP, United Kingdom

CAMBRIDGE UNIVERSITY PRESS
The Edinburgh Building, Cambridge CB2 2RU, United Kingdom
40 West 20th Street, New York, NY 10011-4211, USA
10 Stamford Road, Oakleigh, Melbourne 3166, Australia

Cambridge Reading Teacher's Book 3
Text © Richard Brown and Kate Ruttle 1996
Illustrations © Cambridge University Press 1996

First published 1996

Produced by Gecko Limited, Bicester, Oxon
Printed in the United Kingdom by Scotprint Ltd, Musselburgh, Scotland

A catalogue record for this book is available from the British Library

ISBN 0 521 56995 8

Cover illustration by Ian Newsham

Authors' thanks

For the project

Richard Brown and Kate Ruttle, General Editors of **Cambridge Reading**, would like to extend their warmest thanks to the following.

Annemarie Young, senior commissioning editor of **Cambridge Reading**, for initiating, co-ordinating and developing the project with such skill, dedication and good humour.

Her indispensable team: Sara Ball, Heidi Bradshaw, Leena Chauhan, Jan Closs, Jenny Knight, Deborah Ramsbotham, Frances Reynolds and Julia Strickland.

Jean Glasberg, Consultant Editor, for her invaluable advice and support at every level of the project.

Heather Richards, art buyer, for her skill and flair in finding and encouraging the illustrators for all our books.

All those involved in developing the design and production of the project, particularly Liz Knox, Chris McLeod and his team, Jacqui Chan for Turtle's dance, Jake Tebbit who provided Lexie, and Angela Ashton, Nick Judd, Carrie Long and Andy Wilson at CUP.

Our advisers and reviewers, including Tandy Adlam, Julie Anderson, Richard Andrews, Helen Arnold,

Roger Beard, David Betteridge, Carol Brammer, Joan Brear, Gillian Brown, Kirsty Byrne, Ron Carter, Urszula Clarke, Henrietta Dombey, Ros Fisher, Janet Foden, Prue Goodwin, Alison Littlefair, Barbara Lofthouse, Mary McEvilly, Claire Milne, Jack Ousbey, Lynda Pearce, Katharine Perera, Bridie Raban-Bisby, May Rae, Anne Rowe, Alison Silver, Marie Stacey, Morag Styles, Sue Walker and Marian Whitehead. Their advice and criticism have helped us to think afresh about many issues. We have found this help invaluable, though of course we take full responsibility for all decisions taken.

The many teachers and children in schools around the country who trialled and commented on the books and support materials, for their hard work and thoughtful criticism.

For this book

We are very grateful to Carol Brammer and June Crebbin for their contributions to this book; to Janet Simmonett for her illustrations; and to Graham Portlock for his photographs.

We would also like to extend our thanks to Jenny Knight and Keith Lloyd for their detailed editorial work.

Notice to teachers

The photocopy masters in this publication may be photocopied free of charge for classroom use within the school or institution which purchases the publication. Worksheets and photocopies of them remain the copyright of Cambridge University Press and such photocopies may not be distributed or used in any way outside the purchasing institution. Written permission is necessary if you wish to store the material electronically.

Acknowledgements

We are grateful to the following for permission to reproduce poems or extracts from them: 'Who Is It?' by Theresa Heine, from *A Big Poetry Book*, Blackwell 1989, © Theresa Heine 1989. 'Cats' by Eleanor Farjeon, from *Seeing and Doing*, Thames TV 1977. 'Phew!' by Michael Smith. 'Jacks' by Tony Bradman, first published in Viking Children's Books 1987, Penguin Books Ltd. 'Wings' by Pie Corbett, from *Another First Poetry Book*, ed. John Foster, Oxford University Press, © Pie Corbett 1987.

Contents

PART ONE: Introduction and main components

3 Language study

4 Home–school links

5 Record-keeping and assessment

PART TWO: Teacher's Pages and worksheets

1

PART ONE:

Introduction and main components

1

An overview of *Cambridge Reading*

Learning to read with *Cambridge Reading*

Main features

Cambridge Reading is an innovative series of books and support materials for the teaching of reading throughout the primary years. The books, by both new and established children's writers and illustrators, offer children breadth of choice and a wealth of different writing and illustration styles.

The scheme guides the child from short picture books for sharing, through several developmental phases in reading, to skilled and independent reading of many kinds of text. This is achieved through:

- a balance of different text types and genres which include fiction, non-fiction and poetry;
- a structure which facilitates progress and continuity in the teaching and learning of reading;
- a careful control of language;
- a range of support materials aimed at developing reading skills, including comprehension and knowledge about language;
- an integrated phonics and sight vocabulary programme.

Cambridge Reading meets the requirements of the National Curriculum orders for England and Wales, the Scottish 5–14 Guidelines and the Northern Ireland Common Curriculum. Separate documents which describe these more fully are available from the Educational Marketing Department (tel: 01223–325889).

A clear and flexible structure

- *Cambridge Reading* is structured into five **phases** which reflect the developmental phases in children's reading: Beginning to Read; Becoming a Reader; Towards Independence; Independent Reading; Extended Reading.
- The five phases are divided into **stages** to provide manageable and easily identifiable steps in the children's learning. As teachers record children's development through these stages, they can feel confident that the children are making suitable progress.
- **Sets** of books are linked by theme, author or illustrator. These sets usually overlap more than one stage, and thus allow flexibility and variety in the children's reading pathways.
- **Genre strands**, which are introduced at the second phase, include contemporary stories, fantasy, traditional tales, stories of childhood, poetry and

rhyme, as well as information books. They aim to give children experience of a diversity of writing styles and text types, providing them with a firm foundation for their wider reading.

The *Cambridge Reading* approach

In recent years, understanding of the processes involved in learning to read has developed considerably, leading to a more comprehensive view of the many factors involved.

Approaches like 'look and say', 'phonics' or 'real books' tend to emphasise some aspects of learning to read at the expense of others. *Cambridge Reading*, by contrast, recognises that reading is a multi-layered activity and that success in learning to read will often be influenced – and in some cases determined – by a range of factors. They include:

- the child's motivation to read;
- the quality of the book being read and its appeal to the child;
- the child's understanding of how different kinds of texts work;
- the social context in which the reading takes place;
- the child's prior knowledge of the text;
- the child's engagement with literacy activities related to the text;
- the child's understanding of language patterns and how texts cohere;
- the extent of the child's sight vocabulary;
- the child's skill in using pictorial, semantic, syntactic and phonic cues to decode unknown words.

The quality of the book and the child's motivation to read

Perhaps *the* key factor in reading success is the child's motivation to read, for without it progress will be delayed. To learn to read, young children have to make great efforts. Such efforts need to be rewarded by exciting, funny and appealing stories, by illustrations that add something vital to the story, and by information which is intrinsically interesting. At the heart of *Cambridge Reading* are books that children will really *want* to read and re-read, and which will make reading an enjoyable and rewarding activity.

Understanding how different texts work

Children's understanding of how different kinds of texts work develops from their general experience of books and other texts. To foster this understanding, *Cambridge Reading* provides children, at the outset, with experience of a wide variety of text types, writing styles and illustration approaches.

The social context within which reading takes place

Learning to read is a social activity and children are more likely to make progress if they experience the support and encouragement of reading with others. *Cambridge Reading* promotes the teaching of reading within supportive group and shared reading contexts; many of the texts and materials are designed to be used in these ways.

In the classroom, the child learns to read not only by working with books but also through interacting with the teacher and with classmates.

At home, parents and other family members can share the child's enjoyment of books and can help to develop a positive attitude towards reading.

Prior knowledge of the text

Children will have greater success in reading a text if they have some prior knowledge of its content.

Within *Cambridge Reading*, there are sets of books by the same author and illustrator which, through developing familiarity with particular characters and story settings, allow children to predict events and language patterns.

With information books, discussion of key concepts and vocabulary can help to prepare the children for the book's content.

Literacy activities related to the text

Cambridge Reading provides activities and worksheets around every text, and software for some titles. These activities often require the children to revisit the text in order to carry out tasks which help them to develop their understanding and give them practice in using their growing literacy skills.

Activities on the worksheets ensure that careful attention is paid to print and that cueing strategies develop. They also provide opportunities for children to respond to texts in a variety of ways that develop their spoken-language, listening, writing and reading skills.

Understanding language patterns

In the early phases, particularly the Beginning to Read phase, *Cambridge Reading* provides many texts which have highly patterned language, involving rhythm and rhyme, as well as the repetition of words, phrases and sentences. Such texts are more predictable than straightforward prose and therefore provide additional clues for the beginner reader. They also appeal to children's sense of fun and show that in language there are always opportunities for play.

In other texts, the language used in *Cambridge Reading* has been kept as natural as possible. Characters in the stories say the kinds of things that people do say. This use of everyday language provides the beginner reader, who is already familiar with the world of speech, with familiar and recognisable clues on entering the new world of reading. To this end, writers have not been restricted to a prescribed vocabulary, though they have borne in mind the level of vocabulary and the types of concepts appropriate to a particular age range.

Sight vocabulary and cueing strategies

In the first two phases, *Cambridge Reading* supports the development of children's sight vocabulary through picture books that deploy a sensitive repetition of words and phrases. Fifty of the most commonly used words are taught systematically through workbooks.

Care has been taken in the first two phases to ensure that there is a close match between text and pictures to provide children with good picture cues for their reading.

In addition, there is an extensive, integrated phonics programme to support the development of children's phonological skills.

A note about the logo

The *Cambridge Reading* logo features a leopard called Lexie. She developed from the heraldic leopards in the Cambridge University Press crest, but has a friendlier face and an appealing character. Children will find her appearing on many of the worksheets, offering them suggestions or giving them extra instructions.

A summary of the five phases of *Cambridge Reading*

Beginning to Read (stages A, B)

The books in this phase are intended mainly for children in Reception/Primary 1. During this phase the child will develop:

- concepts of print (e.g. how a book works, voice–print match, constancy of print, left–right orientation);
- the beginnings of a sight vocabulary;
- phonological awareness, including listening skills, appreciation of rhyme, rhythm, alliteration and analogy;
- letter formation and early writing skills;
- a repertoire of familiar stories and rhymes;
- approximate reading, drawing upon memories of the text;
- some accurate reading based largely upon recall of the text;
- an understanding of the relationship between pictures and text.

When young children first start to read, they need books which are motivating and fun, and which build on their existing knowledge of literacy. For many children, nursery rhymes are a good place to start because they have some kind of nursery rhyme book at home and are likely to be familiar with both the rhymes and the idea that they are read. Nursery rhymes for these children are also likely to be associated with the security of home. These are both factors that should help children to read the rhymes successfully.

Five of the Beginning to Read stage A books feature familiar nursery rhymes, and more illustrated rhymes can be found in *The Cambridge Big Book of Nursery Rhymes.*

Many of the other Beginning to Read books are written in rhyme or in highly patterned and memorable language. Having heard these books read aloud, most children are quick to join in with re-readings, enthusiastically chanting the refrains and rapidly memorising the texts.

For children who are confident with rhyming and highly patterned text, there are also Beginning to Read books with less predictable texts. The majority of these books are at the slightly harder Beginning to Read

stage B. These books have a strong story-line and are written in natural language supported by illustrations which help children to predict the text.

The books in the Beginning to Read phase cater flexibly for a wide range of teaching and learning styles, enabling you to select the most appropriate starting points for the children in your class. The most important criterion is that for each child the first experiences of reading should be positive and successful and should motivate them to want to read more. During this phase the teacher will do most of the reading, with the children joining in as they gain familiarity with the texts and confidence in their reading.

Resources to support the Beginning to Read phase

The books

- 12 × 8-page story and rhyme books at stage A
- 3 × 8-page 'undoing a painting' books (non-fiction) at stage A
- 15 × 8-page story and rhyme books at stage B

Support materials

- *Cambridge Reading Teacher's Book 1: Beginning to Read* (including 2 photocopiable worksheets for each book).
- 2 story Big Books, each containing two stories: *A Very Hot Day* and *Walking in the Jungle*; *I Went to School This Morning* and *What For?*
- *The Cambridge Big Book of Nursery Rhymes.*
- *Listening Pictures: First Steps in Phonics* (Flipover Book) with accompanying teacher's guide.
- *Developing a Sight Vocabulary: The First Fifty Words – Workbooks 1, 2* and *3.*
- *Sounds Fun!* (Phonic Games Pack) with accompanying teacher's guide.
- 6 *Cambridge Reading Talking Books* for the computer, with notes for teachers (the stories included are: *A Very Hot Day, The Picnic, Walking in the Jungle, I Went to School This Morning, My Pet* and *What For?*).

Walking in
the Jungle

Richard Brown and Kate Ruttle
Illustrated by Stella Voce

Where's
Woolly?

Bill Gillham
Illustrated by Alex Ayliffe

Hunting in
the Marshes
A Painting

Meredith Hooper

Five Green
Monsters

Juliet Partridge
Illustrated by Stella Voce

I Went to
School This Morning

Richard Brown and Kate Ruttle
Illustrated by Margaret Chamberlain

What's in
the Box?

Bill Gillham
Illustrated by Susie Jenkin-Pearce

Dirty
Dog

Bill Gillham
Illustrated by Alan Snow

A
Very Hot Day

Juliet Partridge
Illustrated by Sami Sweeten

An overview of *Cambridge Reading*　　7

Becoming a Reader (stages A, B, C)

The books in this phase are intended to be mainly for children in Year 1/Primary 2. During this phase, the child:

- learns to read most of a familiar, short and illustrated text aloud;

- continues to share reading of unfamiliar texts;

- is developing a basic sight vocabulary;

- begins to use pictorial, semantic, syntactic and phonic cues to predict unknown words;

- begins to self-correct;

- recalls and discusses some of the main points of the text;

- begins to respond to books through drawing and writing;

- begins to choose their own books.

Once children have made a positive and successful start at reading with the Beginning to Read books, they need to read high-quality and motivating texts to maintain their enthusiasm. At the Becoming a Reader phase, story-lines are more extended and the books are divided into genre strands (contemporary, fantasy, traditional tales, stories of childhood, poetry and rhyme, and information books) so that children can begin to recognise different styles and conventions and develop preferences in their reading.

Within each genre strand there are books at all three of the Becoming a Reader stages, and there are several possible reading pathways for the children to choose from. Some children need the security of a lot of different books at the same level. These children can read all the stage A books regardless of strand, then all the stage B books, and so on. Other children will benefit more from progressing quickly to the challenge of harder books for a while before returning to easier books again. For these children, it is more appropriate to read, or share, all the books in stages A, B and C in one strand before returning to the stage A books in another strand. Both pathways are easily managed within the flexibility of *Cambridge Reading*.

Children who are reading the Becoming a Reader books still need a lot of support in their reading. In all of the books, the illustrations reflect the text very closely, enabling children to make good use of picture cues; the language structures and vocabulary are either natural and familiar or rhyming; and, most importantly, there are strong, often humourous story-lines which make children want to read and re-read them.

Resources to support the Becoming a Reader phase

The books

- 36 story-books

- 9 poetry and rhyme books

- 9 information books

Support materials

- *Cambridge Reading Teacher's Book 2: Becoming a Reader* (including two photocopiable worksheets for each book).

- 2 story Big Books: *Wayne's Box* and *What's the Time?*

- *Cambridge Reading Information Books Teacher's Guide 1: Becoming a Reader.*

- 2 information Big Books: *Dinosaur* and *Bubbles*.

- *Developing a Sight Vocabulary: The First Fifty Words* – Workbooks *4* and *5*.

- *Sounds Fun!* (phonic games pack) with accompanying teacher's guide.

- Software: *SEMERC My World 2* packs to accompany John Prater's fantasy stories and Gerald Rose's traditional tales, with notes for teachers; there will also be *SEMERC Ultima* packs to accompany some of the information books.

Towards Independence
(stages A, B, C)

The books in this phase are intended mainly for children in Years 2 and 3/Primary 3 and 4.

Children who have read successfully, and with enjoyment, through the first two phases of *Cambridge Reading* are now ready to begin to encounter a wider variety of text types and language structures. They are not yet, however, truly independent readers and still benefit from a gradual introduction of more complex and varied language and vocabulary.

The books in the Towards Independence phase are again divided into genre strands and each strand has three books at each of stages A, B and C. By the time they are reading at this phase, most children will be developing preferences for certain types of books. You can encourage this by helping children to select other books from the classroom bookshelf or school library.

As the children read more fluently and easily they also need to build up their reading stamina. The story-books at Towards Independence B and C are all 32 pages long. These are best read straight through although they can be read in small chunks. It is good for children's reading stamina for them to have some experience of sustaining interest and concentration for as long as it takes to read straight through one of these books.

As the children's reading improves, so their reliance on picture cues diminishes. The pictures for the books in the Towards Independence phase still support the text, but the illustrators have been given greater freedom to add more details to the pictures. If you encourage the children to look closely at the pictures, they will often find unexpected details. You can use the pictures as the basis for discussion, story telling and recasting of stories from different points of view.

During this phase the child:

- is learning to read aloud, with expression, from familiar texts, taking punctuation into account;
- is able to read simple unfamiliar texts with some fluency;
- is learning to read silently;
- shares the reading of more demanding books;
- continues to use pictorial, semantic, syntactic and phonic cues to predict unfamiliar words;
- self-corrects when reading;
- can recall and discuss a texts main points;
- is developing the ability to choose books for different purposes;
- is learning to write about, and respond to, texts in a variety of ways.

Resources to support the Towards Independence phase

The books

- 36 story-books in sets of 9 books, divided into 12 books at each of stages A, B and C.
- 9 poetry books, 3 at each of stages A, B and C.
- 9 information books, 3 at each of stages A, B and C.

Support materials

- *Cambridge Reading Teacher's Book 3: Towards Independence* (including two photocopiable worksheets for each book).
- *Cambridge Reading Information Books Teacher's Guide 2: Towards Independence* (including two photocopiable worksheets for each information book).
- 2 information Big Books: *Camouflage* and *Coral Reef*.
- *Phonics for Reading* – photocopiable worksheets, with teacher's notes, to develop spelling patterns from existing phonic knowledge.
- Software: *SEMERC My World 2* packs to support the children's acquisition of writing, editing their work and story telling.
- Cassettes: audio cassettes of the poetry strand and the traditional tales.

Independent and Extended Reading

The books in this phase are intended mainly for children in Years 3–6/Primary 4–7.

These phases extend the development of reading throughout the primary years. There is a growing consensus that children are more likely to become skilled, active and enthusiastic readers if they are consistently challenged, informed and entertained by the books they read. The books in the Independent Reading and Extended Reading phases build on the expertise, knowledge and enthusiasm for reading that children have gained through the earlier phases of *Cambridge Reading*; and the accompanying support material helps children to explore and reflect upon a variety of reading experiences.

The Treasure Cave
Rosemary Hayes
Illustrated by
Ian Newsham

Dad's Promise
Richard Brown
Illustrated by Anthony Lewis

Coyote Girl
Rosalind Kerven
Illustrated by Amanda Hall

Snow in the Kitchen
Richard Brown
Illustrated by Amanda Harvey

Knickerbocker Number Nine
Poems chosen by
Richard Brown and Kate Ruttle
Illustrated by
John Bendall-Brunello and Sarah McDonald

Out and About
Poems chosen by
Richard Brown and Kate Ruttle
Illustrated by
Amanda Harvey and Lisa Kopper

Cutting and Sticking
June Crebbin
Illustrated by Peter Kavanagh

Dancing to the River
Grace Hallworth
Illustrated by Alex Ayliffe

A variety of literary genres and text types is provided throughout **Cambridge Reading**. In the Becoming a Reader and Towards Independence phases the books are organised into six strands.

Contemporary
Stories by Tony Bradman or June Crebbin

These are stories set in the present which do not include any obvious elements of fantasy and which reflect the patterns of everyday life.

Fantasy
Stories by John Prater or Rosemary Hayes

In these stories, characters, events and locations are in invented worlds or break the natural laws of the universe.

Traditional Tales
Stories by Gerald Rose,
Joanna Troughton, Rosalind Kerven and others

Drawing upon the world's rich store of myths and legends, fables, folk and fairy tales, these are imaginative retellings in contemporary language of traditional tales from many countries.

Stories of Childhood
Stories retold by Richard Brown and others

Fifteen individuals (including Gerald Rose and Grace Hallworth) retell the story of a significant event in their childhood. Most of these autobiographical stories have been retold by Richard Brown.

Poetry and Rhyme
Edited by Richard Brown and Kate Ruttle

This strand includes nursery rhymes, riddles, free verse, new poems and traditional favourites, as well as poems in translation and from many different cultures.

Information Books
By Meredith Hooper or Phil Gates

Factual writing is presented in a variety of ways to motivate children to read for information and to give them an early experience of the different purposes, presentation and language of non-fiction texts. (There are separate teacher's guides to accompany the information books.)

The support materials

Cambridge Reading provides a range of materials to help you support children's progress in reading. Some materials are designed to be used with the whole class or with a group. Others are for individual use (e.g. the worksheets and workbooks), although the learning context may be a group one.

The pupil's support material develops and consolidates the children's reading skills and understanding through tasks which usually require them to revisit the book. The support material includes:

Big Books

These provide texts in a size that is big enough for the teacher to give large groups of children a shared experience of the same text and to demonstrate early reading skills and strategies.

Photocopiable worksheets (see pp. 77–212)

Each book is accompanied by two worksheets which provide activities to develop reading or phonic skills, as well as the opportunity for children to respond personally to the stories. The worksheets for each book are accompanied by a page of teacher's notes.

Phonics for Reading (see p. 33)

This is a photocopiable resource book containing worksheets designed to develop spelling patterns from existing phonic knowledge.

Listening Pictures: First Steps in Phonics (Flipover Book)

This is intended mainly for use with children in Reception/Primary 1. It provides a structured bank of pictures to help you develop children's early phonological awareness. There is an accompanying teacher's guide.

Sounds Fun! (Phonic Games Pack)

This is intended mainly for use with children in Reception/Primary 1 and Year 1/Primary 2, although it can also be used with older children who are experiencing difficulties. The games reinforce early phonic skills including alliteration (initial sounds), rhyming, and word-building using onset and rime. The equipment is versatile and is appropriate for children working at different stages. *Sounds Fun!* is accompanied by a teacher's guide.

Sight vocabulary workbooks

Developing a Sight Vocabulary: The First Fifty Words is a set of five workbooks in which children can learn to recognise and to write 50 of the most common words which they encounter in their reading. Each of the words is taught within the context of pictures and sentences taken from the books in the first two phases of *Cambridge Reading*.

Computer software

Cambridge Reading Talking Books

Six of the books in the Beginning to Read phase have been reproduced for the computer, with sound and animation. They are accompanied by a guide for teachers.

SEMERC My World 2 packs

Some of the books from the Becoming a Reader phase onwards are supported by this versatile software which enables children to compose their own pictures using characters from the books and then to add their own text with the help of the word bank provided. The inclusion of line drawings enables you to make your own additional worksheets and enables the children to create drawings that can be coloured in. (Schools will need to own SEMERC's *My World 2* in order to use the *My World 2* screens.) They are accompanied by a guide for teachers.

SEMERC Ultima packs

Some of the information books (Becoming a Reader phase onwards) are supported by Ultima packs, enabling you to differentiate the amount of information children are asked to read. The easier levels of text mirror those in the book, but additional information is also available for more able readers and for children working with adult supervision. Digitised speech is used to support early reading levels. (Schools do not need any other software to run the Ultima packs.)

Cassettes

The poetry strand and the traditional tales, which often have their roots in the oral tradition, are available on audio cassette. On both cassettes male and female actors from a variety of world cultures read the texts clearly.

The cassettes can be used in a number of ways, for example:

- to introduce a text to a group or class of children;
- for small groups of children to listen together before discussing the text;
- to model good reading;
- simply to enjoy.

When a cassette recording of a text is available, this is indicated by the cassette symbol on the Teacher's Page.

Bridging books

The transition from the Becoming a Reader phase to the Towards Independence phase may prove too big a step for some children. To help these children bridge the gap, additional sets of books are provided. Each set of bridging books begins with books which are a little easier than Becoming a Reader: C, and then gradually moves the children on to books of equivalent difficulty to Towards Independence: A. All the bridging books are in full colour and are motivating and fun to read. Each set is accompanied by a teacher's book containing notes and appropriate support material.

Photocopiable material for parents (see pp. 53–58)

Cambridge Reading recognises the importance of home support, especially when a child is learning to read. A specimen photocopiable letter for parents, an advisory leaflet and a Home Reading Record are provided.

Photocopiable records (see pp. 39–50, 62–70)

A variety of photocopiable record-keeping formats is provided to help you keep track of the children's progress.

2

Towards Independence

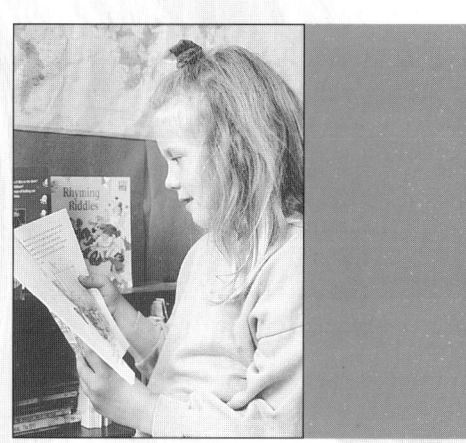

An index of the books at stages A, B and C

Strand/Stage	Title (in alphabetical order)	Author	Teacher's Page
Stories of Childhood	Ben's Amazing Birthday	Richard Brown	159
A	Dad's Promise	Richard Brown	162
	Tulips for Dad	Richard Brown	165
	A Welsh Lamb	Richard Brown	168
B	Dancing in Soot	Richard Brown	171
	The Haystack	Richard Brown	174
	A Shoot of Corn	Richard Brown	177
C	Snow in the Kitchen	Richard Brown	180
	The Watch by the Sea	Richard Brown	183
Poetry	In the Mirror	Richard Brown and Kate Ruttle	186
A	Marvel Paws	Richard Brown and Kate Ruttle	189
	Nonsense!	Richard Brown and Kate Ruttle	192
	A Corner of Magic	Richard Brown and Kate Ruttle	195
B	A Lick of the Spoon	Richard Brown and Kate Ruttle	198
	Knickerbocker Number Nine	Richard Brown and Kate Ruttle	201
	A Mosquito in the Cabin	Richard Brown and Kate Ruttle	204
C	Out and About	Richard Brown and Kate Ruttle	207
	Welcome Night	Richard Brown and Kate Ruttle	210
Information Books	(see *Cambridge Reading Information Books Teacher's Guide 2*)		
	Animal Communication	Phil Gates	
A	Camouflage	Phil Gates	
	Codes and Signals	Phil Gates	
	A Book of Hours	Meredith Hooper	
B	Noah's Ark	Meredith Hooper	
	The Tomb of Nebamun	Meredith Hooper	
	Coral Reef	Meredith Hooper	
C	Desert	Meredith Hooper	
	Rainforest	Meredith Hooper	

About the books

For the Towards Independence phase there are:
- 36 story-books
- 9 poetry anthologies
- 9 information books.

In addition there are two information Big Books:
- *Camouflage*
- *Coral Reef*.

The phase is divided into three stages of difficulty: A, B and C.

There is a gradual progression in the demands made at each stage in terms of:
- text length
- structure
- language
- vocabulary
- concepts.

There are six strands – contemporary, fantasy, traditional tales, stories of childhood, poetry and information books. There are nine books in each strand, three at each of the stages A, B and C.

The strands

Contemporary

All these stories (written by June Crebbin and illustrated by Peter Kavanagh) are about two families who live next to each other and are friends. The stories are about special events in their lives – for example, strawberry picking, a dog show, a concert, house decorating, a pyjama party, a wedding; and some feature animals that assume special significance – for example, a talking parrot, a lost kitten, a dog that tries to sing.

Stage A
- Cutting and Sticking
- Parrot Talk
- Strawberry Picking

Stage B
- The Dog Show
- The Pyjama Party
- The Special Cake

Stage C
- A Cat for Keeps
- Don't Be Late!
- Spike and the Concert

Fantasy

Drawing upon elements of legend, fairy stories, science-fiction, the supernatural and fantasy, these stories (written by Rosemary Hayes and illustrated by Ian Newsham) are full of humour, action and surprise. They take the reader into many different worlds and unusual adventures. Four of the stories have a recurring character, Mr Mulch, whose powers include making children invisible or tiny and turning a vegetable patch into a jungle.

Stage A
- The Big Shrink
- The Grabbing Bird
- The Treasure Cave

Stage B
- Jumble Power
- The Magic Sword
- The Peace Ring

Stage C
- The Amazing Mr Mulch
- Mr Mulch's Magic Mixtures
- The Slippery Planet

Traditional Tales

These are imaginative retellings of traditional stories in a variety of language styles, and draw upon the world's rich store of myths and legends, folk and fairy tales, and fables. They are written by Antonia Barber, Grace Hallworth, Rosalind Kerven and others, with illustrations in a range of different styles by various illustrators, some reflecting specific cultures.

Stage A
- Dancing to the River *Caribbean*
- How the Animals Got Their Tails *Aboriginal*
- Rabbit's Tail *Scottish*

Stage B
- The Lord Mount Dragon *Irish*
- The Weather Drum *Siberian*
- Volcano Woman *South Pacific*

Stage C
- Coyote Girl *Hopi Indian*
- The Cape of Rushes *English*
- The Most Beautiful Child *Hindu*

Stories of Childhood

These are nine autobiographical stories from a variety of backgrounds and periods. All are based on childhood memories and are retold by Richard Brown. There are various illustrators.

Stage A

- Ben's Amazing Birthday
- Dad's Promise
- Tulips for Dad

Stage B

- A Welsh Lamb
- Dancing in Soot
- The Haystack

Stage C

- A Shoot of Corn
- Snow in the Kitchen
- The Watch by the Sea

Poetry

The nine thematically organised poetry anthologies are chosen by Richard Brown and Kate Ruttle. There are various illustrators. The theme of each is shown in italics.

Stage A

- In the Mirror
  Myself
- Marvel Paws
  Pets
- Nonsense!
  Nonsense rhymes

Stage B

- A Corner of Magic
  Story poems
- A Lick of the Spoon   *Food*
- Knickerbocker Number Nine
  Games and leisure activities

Stage C

- A Mosquito in the Cabin
  Minibeasts
- Out and About
  Outdoors
- Welcome Night
  Night

Information Books

Stage A books are written by Phil Gates, stage B and C books are by Meredith Hooper. Each book is designed to present a particular topic that will appeal to children and hold their interest.

Factual writing is presented in a variety of stimulating ways to motivate children to read information and to give them experience of the different purposes, presentation and language of non-fiction. (See *Cambridge Reading Information Books Teacher's Guide 2: Towards Independence* for guidance on using these books.)

Stage A

- Animal Communication
- Camouflage
- Codes and Signals

Stage B

- A Book of Hours
- Noah's Ark
- The Tomb of Nebamun

Stage C

- Coral Reef
- Desert
- Rainforest

Covers and title pages

The names of the author and illustrator are printed on the cover of each book. However, the text of some of the books may not be entirely the original work of the author. Some are based on traditional songs, rhymes, stories, etc. For these books, the name of the author is repeated on the title page inside the book with the words:

- *adapted by* (which means that it is based on the traditional version, but has been slightly altered);
- *retold by* (which means that there are no accepted definitive words for the story and the author has chosen the words in which to retell the story);
- *chosen by* (which means that the author has selected writing from traditional or acknowledged sources and reproduced it without change).

Using the books

Children at the Towards Independence phase will benefit from a range of reading experiences: listening to text, talking about it, sharing the reading of it, reading it to themselves, and responding to it through language activities. The emphasis at this phase, however, is the development of the children's independence in reading: choosing their own books, reading independently, responding to books at a personal level, and widening their experience of text-types and genres.

Talking about the book

Talking about the book before, during and after a reading of it helps to orientate the children to its theme, subject matter, language and style. *Before reading*, talking about the book will help them make predictions about the content and create anticipation. *During a reading*, talking about the book will help clarify what is happening or what is implied and it will encourage the children to respond to the content, sometimes with questions of their own. *After reading*, discussion develops the skills of review and reflection.

Sharing reading

Although children at this phase will be able to read the books with a large measure of independence, much can still be gained by sharing some of the books with the child – or a group of children – before they enjoy the book on their own. The child can:

- listen as the adult reads;
- echo and discuss unfamiliar words;
- read simultaneously;
- take over some of the reading;
- read the part of one of the characters;
- share the book in a group;
- discuss the text.

Text types and genres

At this phase you can begin to help the children towards an understanding of how genres differ and of the differences between story, poetry and information. Point out to the children that the stories can be divided into reality or fantasy:

- The stories by June Crebbin reflect events that could happen in real life; those in the autobiographical strand retold by Richard Brown really did happen.
- The stories by Rosemary Hayes are full of invented happenings, creatures and objects which would not be met in real life.
- The traditional stories are very old and share many of the characteristics of fantasy.

Once you have introduced the concepts of reality and fantasy, you can:

- ask the children to find other examples of each category, drawing upon the classroom's stock of picture and story-books;
- help the children to classify some of the poems in the poetry anthologies in the same way;
- talk about the differences in form and purpose of story, poetry and information, using the books in the scheme.

Responding to books

Once the children have enjoyed a book in a group or independently, they can extend their understanding of it through language activities. At this phase, activities and worksheets are supplied to help the children develop:

- comprehension (to check and extend understanding);
- vocabulary;
- personal response (to link themes, events and feelings in the stories to their own lives, and to express opinions about the texts).

Not only are these kinds of activities important to the development of literacy, they also require the children to revisit the books with specific reading purposes in mind, ensuring a deeper understanding of the text.

Using the poetry books

The nine poetry anthologies and the accompanying cassettes offer children a broad introduction to poetry. A large number of poets have been included and each book has a theme. Some of the poems are established favourites, others deserve to be better known, and there are many newly published poems. The collections encompass a range of different forms, styles and cultures which invite different responses. The shorter collections can be read from cover to cover if you or the child wish; the longer collections are best dipped into. They can be used in the same contexts as the other books: read aloud to the class or group, discussed and explored in group reading sessions, and shared one-to-one at home as well as at school. The two worksheets which accompany each book follow the same pattern as those for the story-books, concentrating on reading development and personal response. They either focus on one poem or on the book's theme and are offered as examples of the many ways in which children can engage with the poem or the book.

Poetry is rich in opportunities for developing knowledge about language. The following teaching points and activities are general suggestions for developing language work and they can be used instead of or in conjunction with the worksheets. They can be applied as appropriate to any of the anthologies.

Themes

The books' themes are:

Stage A   Myself *(In the Mirror)*
          Pets *(Marvel Paws)*
          Nonsense rhymes *(Nonsense!)*

Stage B   Stories *(A Corner of Magic)*
          Food *(A Lick of the Spoon)*
          Games and leisure activities
          (Knickerbocker Number Nine)

Stage C   Minibeasts *(A Mosquito in the Cabin)*
          Outdoors *(Out and About)*
          Night *(Welcome Night)*

The books' themes can be explored simply through word-webs. A word-web can be brainstormed with the children before the theme is experienced through the poems. After reading some or all of the poems together, another word-web can be constructed to reflect what was in the collection. The example below is a word-web reflecting what is in *In the Mirror*.

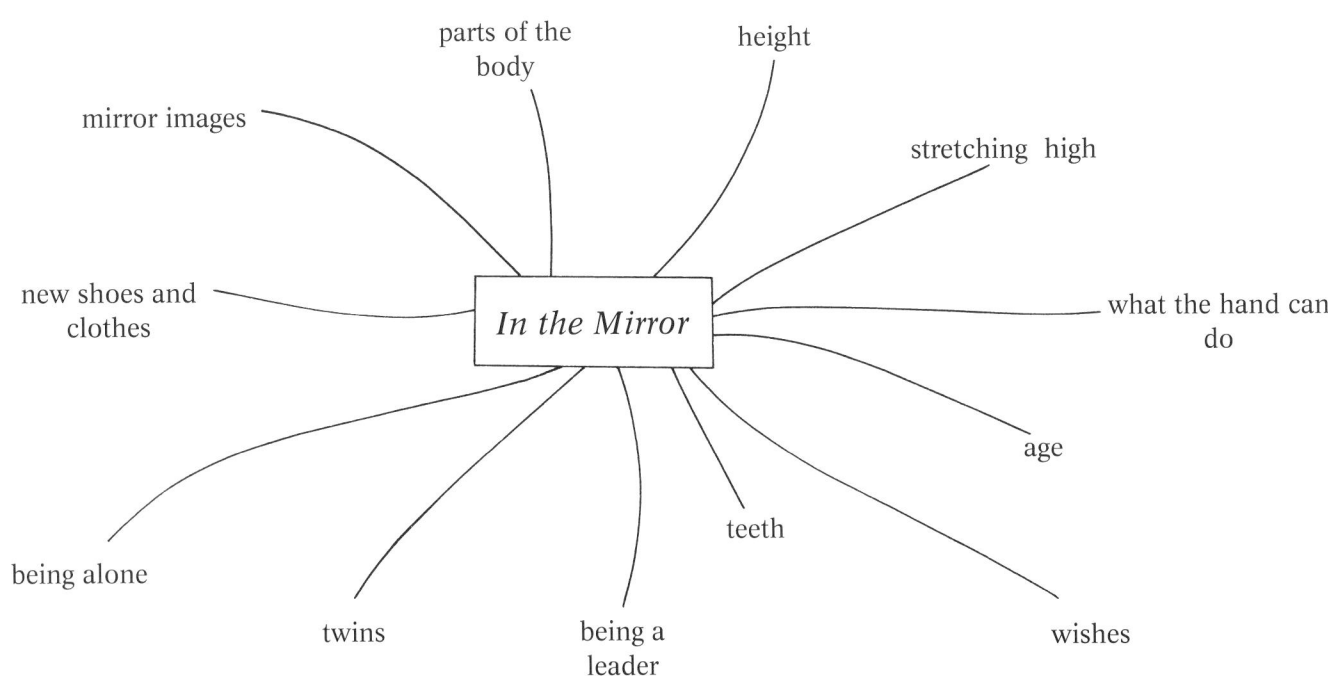

The two word-webs can then be compared. Where they differ, subjects for poems by the children themselves could be suggested.

Other poems on the same theme could also be collected by the children in the course of their reading. If there are enough poems, they could be read on tape by you and/or the children as an extra thematic response to be shared in class.

Modelling responses

By watching how you respond to poetry, children learn a lot about how to respond themselves. There are many different ways to respond to a poem beyond simply reading it aloud and asking the children what they thought it was about and whether they liked it. Some suggestions are set out below under key headings.

Exploring meaning

- Before reading the poem, comment on its title and illustration, showing how both create anticipation and give clues to what the poem is about.

- After reading the poem, return to the title and illustration and discuss their appropriateness.

- Read the poem aloud in a tone and pace suitable for the poem, keeping your voice natural. Avoid using a special 'poetic' voice.

- After the first reading, comment on how you read the poem, what gave you clues about how it should be read and what you would change. Use the vocabulary appropriate to this; for example, pause, pace, rhythm, emphasis. Then re-read it aloud with these points in mind. This will help children to develop their own read-aloud skills.

  Alternatively, play the taped version of the poem and comment in a similar way on the reader's approach to the poem, replaying the tape to illustrate your points.

- Look at any puzzling, hidden or ambiguous meanings in the poem in an exploratory way, inviting the children to give their ideas by using such open questions as:
    - I wonder what that bit's about . . . ?
    - How does he or she feel here?
    - How do we know that?
    - How does this bit make you feel? Why?

- Focus on important images in the poem. Help the children to do this by asking them to close or turn over their books and say what image from the poem stays in their mind. Ask the children to describe the image. (Bear in mind that some children are poor visualisers and may find this activity difficult.)

- If the poem tells a story or has events in it, get the children to retell the poem as a story.

- When poems suggest accompanying movements (e.g. mime) or parts for more than one voice (e.g. chants, refrains) help the children by demonstrating what should be done. After they have completed the activity, give them constructive feedback.

Vocabulary

- Draw children's attention to particular words and phrases that you think are used well in the poem or that particularly interest you. Discuss what you like about them.

- Ask the children to do the same.

- Give the children the opportunity to highlight and discuss words they are not familiar with. Help them to use the context in which the word is used to find its meaning. Use dictionaries to check, if appropriate.

- Explore synonyms of words used in poems and occasionally see what happens when you substitute these for words in the poem.

Exploring form

In talking about how poems are written (i.e. their form) you can introduce the children to the appropriate vocabulary; for example, verses, free verse, line lengths and breaks, rhyme, rhythm, sound values (alliteration, soft and hard sounds).

When discussing a poem you could, if appropriate, draw children's attention to the following elements of form.

Verses

- Some are regularly patterned (e.g. in couplets or quatrains).

- Some are irregular in length.

- Some rhyme, some don't.

- Some use a traditional form such as a haiku.

- Some help to sequence events or images and highlight meaning.

- Some poems don't have verses.

Free verse

- The poet chooses not to use a given verse form but lets the poem shape itself.
- It may or may not be divided into verses.

Line lengths and breaks

- The length of the line may be determined by its beat or by its meaning.
- Breaks sometimes provide pauses and emphasise the first word or phrase in the next line.

Rhyme

- Rhyming patterns can be pointed out in the first verse, letting the children spot the same pattern in succeeding verses.
- This could include internal rhymes (i.e. a rhyming pair in the same line).
- Rhyming poetry can be compared with unrhyming poetry to bring out the essential differences in sound and pattern.

Rhythm

- Pronounced rhythms can be beaten out with the children, the fingers of one hand tapping the side of the other hand (or soft clapping can be used).
- Syllables and stress can be explained.
- The children can be asked if a poem which does not use a metrical form has a rhythm of its own.

Sound values

- You can draw the children's attention to examples of alliteration and patterns of sound if these are used to particular effect (e.g. 'The speckled air of summer stars').

Writing

- Form can be explained and understood through the children's own poetry writing. Use the framework of a poem they have just enjoyed for the children's poem, for example:

    When I was One,

    I . . .

    When I was Two,

    I . . .

- Themes can be explored through the children's own poems.

Preferences

One of the aims of poetry teaching is to help children develop preferences for particular poems, kinds of poems and poets. In the process the children should begin to give reasons for their preferences. They can be helped to do this by:

- encouraging them to choose a poem that they particularly like from an anthology already shared – they can read it aloud to the other children and say why they chose it and what they think is good about it;
- learning favourite poems by heart;
- writing, or word processing, favourite poems and collecting them in a class or personal anthology;
- taking poems home to share with the family;
- illustrating poems;
- making poetry cards, the poem on one side of the card and an illustration on the other, for display in the classroom.

Suggested reading pathways

Having achieved a degree of independence, the children should be encouraged to choose their own books, with guidance as appropriate. Within the scheme there are two main pathways to choose between: the 'linear' or the 'zigzag'.

The linear pathway

This is a traditional approach to progression in reading schemes. The child reads all or most of the books at stage A before proceeding to stage B and then to C. Some advantages of this approach are:

- It is easier to manage in the classroom.
- It is easier to monitor progression.
- The children achieve a measure of fluency and independence at one stage before progressing to the next.
- Children can still return to favourite books at an earlier stage to demonstrate their developing skills.
- Parents, and other adult helpers, have a clearer idea of the child's reading attainment.

However, there are disadvantages:

- Some children can stay too long at one stage.
- Inequalities in reading skills between children become more apparent, sometimes having an adverse effect on children who are making slower progress.
- It narrows the range of books children can experience.
- It does not allow a child to follow through a set of nine books to its conclusion.

- It prompts parents and other adult helpers simply to hear the child read rather than to share the book with them or to read it aloud.

The zigzag pathway

The zigzag pathway is for more confident readers. Children following a zigzag pathway will experience all nine books in one strand before moving onto another strand. For example, they might follow the pathway shown in the diagram below.

Some of the advantages of a zigzag pathway are:

- It reflects more closely the way the children develop as readers at this early stage; that is, through listening to, and sharing, a text before attempting to read it independently.
- It provides for the needs of children who are progressing quickly and need greater challenges in their reading.
- Children can use their growing familiarity with characters, themes, setting, art work and authorial voice to help them tackle harder texts more confidently.
- Shared reading of the books at harder stages allows the children to develop a greater range of reading skills.
- It encourages children to return to easier books to practise their reading skills and to increase their fluency and confidence.
- It allows you and the parent to share a greater range of books with the child.

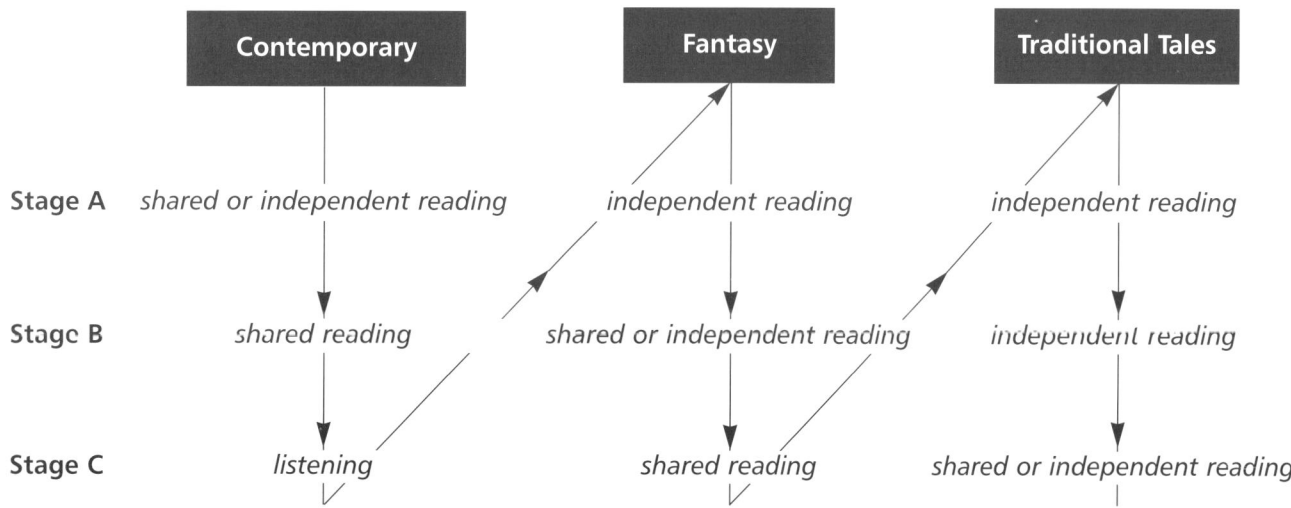

The zigzag pathway.

The disadvantages might include:

- It is harder to manage. Instead of simply hearing a child read from a familiar book, you or the parent have to be clear whether the book the child is 'reading' is to be read independently, shared or just listened to.

- You have to ensure that the child is experiencing books equally in these three different ways.

- Some parents may have difficulty in understanding the approach – they may complain that a book is 'too hard' or 'too easy' or 'they've had it before'.

To help you overcome these potential difficulties, there is a child's individual record where you can mark whether each book has been shared or read independently (p. 62).

Preparing for the next phase: Independent Reading A and B

Whichever pathway the child follows at the Towards Independence phase, it is desirable that they achieve fluency and confidence before progressing to the next phase, Independent Reading. This can be assessed by asking the child to read aloud to you from an unfamiliar Towards Independence stage C book. Use Reading Record 2: Hearing a child read, on page 64, to help you record what you observe about the child's performance.

If you feel that the child is not quite ready to progress to the next phase you can:

- encourage the child to re-read favourite or familiar books, both within **Cambridge Reading** and from other sources;

- review the child's reading records to identify any specific reading problems that need immediate attention.

Group reading

Children can support each other's reading development in supervised small group-reading sessions. The following sequence is recommended:

- Make sure that every child can see a copy of the book.

- Share the book in the ways you have already modelled so that the children can join in, focus on aspects of the print and become familiar with the text.

- More independent readers can share the reading; for example, by taking narrator and character parts. They should note words they find difficult so they can be discussed later.

- If a cassette of the story or the poems is available, it can be listened to, the children following the text in the book at the same time or during a second reading.

- After the reading, you can ask each child to contribute an observation, a question or an opinion about the text which they would like to share with the group. These can be written down first or they can be more spontaneous. They can form the basis of the discussion about the book before a worksheet is selected.

- If appropriate, select one of the worksheets for the children to complete, or give them a choice of which they would like to do. They are intended to read the worksheet themselves. You may need to model the first part of the activity with them. Talk about the children's responses to the worksheet at the end of the session.

- If possible, give the children the opportunity to take the book home.

- Keep a record using Reading Record 1: Books read and worksheets completed (see p. 62).

Using the Teacher's Page and the worksheets

Every book in the Towards Independence phase is supported by two worksheets and a page of notes for teachers (see pp. 77–212).

Worksheet activities help children to develop:

- reading comprehension
- sequencing
- vocabulary
- writing for different purposes
- understanding of text structure
- personal response.

The Teacher's Page explains the purpose of each worksheet and the best ways of using it. It also suggests points to highlight before, during or after reading the book.

Using the worksheets

Worksheet 1 is concerned with general reading development. Worksheet 2 helps children to develop a personal response to books and poems. An index listing the skills practised in the worksheets is given on page 28.

The instructions on the worksheets are intended to be read by the children themselves. The text is based on the words and pictures from the book.

It is not intended that *every* child will use *every* worksheet. Worksheets need to be selected on the basis of each child's need. In practice, this may mean that children who make rapid progress in reading will need to complete fewer of the reading development worksheets. Others, who need more support, may need to work through one or both worksheets for almost every book they share. The majority of children are likely to fall somewhere in between.

The worksheets are best used in the context of supervised small-group work. Most of the activities on the worksheets require the children to refer to the book while engaged in the task. To facilitate this it may be helpful to keep together small sets of books with photocopies of the relevant worksheets.

You can easily keep track of which worksheets a child has completed by using Reading Record 1, supplied on page 62.

An index of skills developed by the worksheets

Strand/Stage		Title	Worksheet 1 – Reading development	Worksheet 2 – Personal response
Contemporary		Cutting and Sticking	Comprehension and recall	Exploring a character's emotions
	A	Parrot Talk	Comprehension: answering questions	Extension of ideas
		Strawberry Picking	Matching and ordering sentences	Relating text to personal experience
		The Dog Show	Comprehension: answering questions	Ranking sentences
	B	The Pyjama Party	Bookmaking and illustration	Exploring a character's emotions
		The Special Cake	Sequencing and cloze	Inventing a cake
		A Cat for Keeps	Classification	Completing an attributes chart
	C	Don't Be Late!	Sequencing events to make a game	Relating text to personal experience
		Spike and the Concert	Finding information; writing captions	Exploring a character's actions
Fantasy		The Big Shrink	Sequencing events to create a game	Ranking events: pictures and sentences
	A	The Grabbing Bird	Comprehension: crossword	Exploring characters' emotions
		The Treasure Cave	Classification: descriptions	Choosing an exciting plot point
		Jumble Power	Labelling; word grid; syllables	Inventing a machine; labelling
	B	The Magic Sword	Cloze: vocabulary extension	Exploring characters' reactions
		The Peace Ring	Cloze: vocabulary extension	Explanatory writing
		Mr Mulch's Magic Mixtures	Making a riddle game; matching text and pictures	Inventing a magic mixture; labelling
	C	The Amazing Mr Mulch	Finding information; sequencing events	Ranking in order of preference
		The Slippery Planet	Cloze: sequencing; bookmaking	Inventing a space creature
Traditional Tales		Dancing to the River	Comprehension: crossword	Writing a song
	A	How the Animals Got Their Tails	Cloze; sequencing	Inventing an animal; word play
		Rabbit's Tail	Classification: descriptions	Problem solving
		The Lord Mount Dragon	Exploring a character's emotions	Ranking events
	B	The Weather Drum	Sequencing; bookmaking	Extension of ideas
		Volcano Woman	Completing descriptions; drawing	Relating text to personal experience
		Coyote Girl	Comprehension and classification	Ranking events
	C	The Cape of Rushes	Finding synonyms	Relating text to personal experience
		The Most Beautiful Child	Bookmaking and illustrating	Relating text to personal experience
Stories of Childhood		Ben's Amazing Birthday	Cloze: vocabulary extension	Writing a report
	A	Dad's Promise	Classification: vocabulary extension	Relating text to personal experience
		Tulips for Dad	Comprehension: crossword	Alternative plot lines
		A Welsh Lamb	Cloze; matching pictures and text	Relating text to personal experience
	B	Dancing in Soot	Cloze: vocabulary extension	Writing reports
		The Haystack	Comprehension: true/false	Writing a report
		A Shoot of Corn	Cloze; sequencing	Exploring a character's emotions
	C	Snow in the Kitchen	Cloze: vocabulary extension	Relating text to personal experience
		The Watch by the Sea	Exploring a character's emotions	Relating text to personal experience
Poetry		In the Mirror	Labelling	Drawing: wishes
	A	Marvel Paws	Sequencing	Classifying; ranking in order of preference
		Nonsense!	Cloze; sequencing; matching	Choosing favourite poems
		A Corner of Magic	Cloze: vocabulary extension	Extension of own ideas
	B	A Lick of the Spoon	Finding information; using quotations	Writing a poem
		Knickerbocker Number Nine	Rhyming cloze; sequencing	Writing a poem
		A Mosquito in the Cabin	Alliteration	Extension of own ideas: tabulating
	C	Out and About	Sequencing using rhyme	Relating a poem to personal experience
		Welcome Night	Sentence completion; vocabulary extension	Relating poems to personal experience

How to use the Teacher's Page

A facsimile of the front cover to make identification of the book easy.

Information about the book and links with other books at the same stage.

...portant ...ncepts and ...eas the ...ildren will ...ed to ...derstand ...appreciate ...e book ...ly.

...ints to bear ...mind while ...ading the ...ok. Can ...clude good ...aces to stop ...d invite ...ediction or ...mment.

How the Animals Got Their Tails

Told by Mona Green
Edited by Pamela Lofts

Illustrator Grace Fielding

Strand traditional tales

Towards Independence: A

Other books in the strand at this stage
- Dancing to the River
- Rabbit's Tail

Introducing the book
- Talk about the cover, including the title and blurb. Invite predictions about the book's contents.
- Explain that this is a traditional tale, told by the Aboriginal people, the native inhabitants of Australia. This version was told to Pamela Lofts, who is Australian, by Mona Green, who is an Aboriginal woman. The writer has kept closely to what she was told and how she was told it.
- Tell the children the pictures have been painted by an Aboriginal artist, based on traditional dot art.

Using the book
- Be prepared for the children to meet unfamiliar words. Help them to work out what the words mean by using the context and pictures.

- Explain that a corroboree is a special meeting of Aboriginal people during which stories are told and songs and dances are performed. Sometimes it lasts for a few days and nights.

After reading the book
- Ask the children if they are familiar with other creation myths which offer an explanation about why things are as they are now. Examples are Kipling's *Just So Stories* and Joanna Troughton's picture books in Becoming a Reader C. See also *The Weather Drum* (stage B).
- The children may like to invent and illustrate their own creation myths.

Ideas for discussion and points you may wish to share with the children.

WORKSHEET 1
Reading Development

Activity *Cloze; sequencing*
- Make sure the children can read all of the words they will need to choose from to complete the cloze.
- Some children may need to write the words on slips of paper first and move them around the cloze to find the right places for them. Then they can copy the answers in.
- Once they have finished, they can check their answers by looking at pages 8 and 9 of the book.
- For the drawing and writing task, ask the children to concentrate on the next important or dramatic point in the story. They will need to refer back to the book to help them choose this.

WORKSHEET 2
Personal Response

Activity *Inventing an animal; word play*
- Ask the children to look at the pictures of animals with the tails they originally had (page 4). See if they can identify each animal.
- Discuss the task on the worksheet. Explain that the children can choose tails that make very strange animals if they like.
- Introduce the idea of making a new word by combining existing words.

Extension activities
- Make a list of animals and encourage the children to suggest new animals by combining different features of two animals (e.g. a 'tiraffe' could be a long-necked tiger, a 'crocaroo' could be a bouncing crocodile).
- The children could make a class book of new animals, drawing and labelling each one.

These boxes explain the purpose of the worksheets and give any information you may need to ensure that the children complete the activities. They also contain ideas for extending the work, when appropriate.

Linking reading and writing

The links between reading and writing are increasingly important as children's literacy skills develop.

In *Cambridge Reading* these links are fostered in a number of ways.

Worksheets

Most of the worksheets require the children to write. The writing varies from a few words to full stories and poems, but in each case the children are presented with a clear reason for writing and a framework that supports and guides their writing. Through these activities children learn to recognise different aspects of the structure of the stories they read, and begin to transfer this awareness to their own writing.

Bookmaking

Several of the worksheets ask the children to make little books. Photocopiable instructions for making the books are given on pages 31–32. The same instructions can be used for making blank books in which the children can retell or adapt stories from the *Cambridge Reading* books. Bookmaking is a very effective way of encouraging children to read because:

- children feel a sense of ownership of books which they have made and therefore are willing to read and re-read them;

- the books can be adapted by the children to provide a new reading experience based on a familiar text (see suggestions below);

- the work involved in making books can be differentiated to enable children to complete them at the most appropriate level.

Home-made books can be used to re-create texts in a number of ways. Some suggestions are given on page 33.

Folded booklet

You can make and illustrate your own booklet from
some of the worksheets in **Cambridge Reading**.
Follow these instructions to make your own folded booklet.

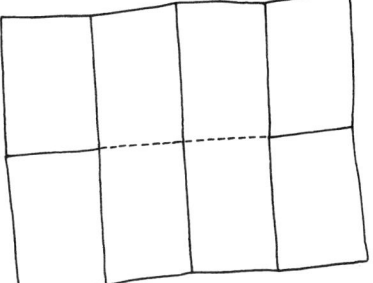

1. Fold the worksheet into eight rectangles.

2. Cut through the middle along the line of dashes.

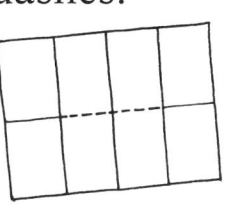 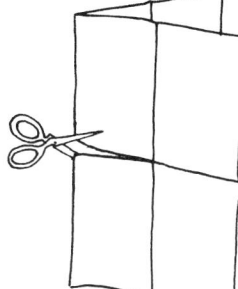

3. Fold the paper like this.

4. Push left and right to make a cube . . .

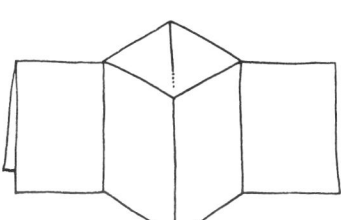

5. . . . then a cross.

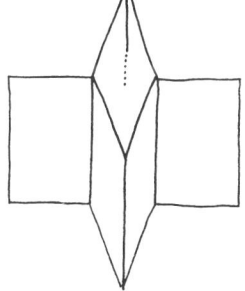

6. Fold around to make the booklet.

7. Add the illustrator's name and the price.

You can make your own folded booklet.
Choose a story you would like to write and draw.

Strip booklet

Some of the stories in *Cambridge Reading* are printed on the worksheets in strips. You can make these into a book. Follow these instructions.

1. Cut up the strips that make up the story.

2. Put the strips in the right order.

3. Add a card cover if you wish.

4. Staple the strips together like this.

5. Add your own pictures if there is space for them.

6. Write a title, the name of the author and a blurb.

You can make your own strip booklet. Choose a story you would like to write and draw.

Sequencing the story

If the children can identify the main plot points from the story, they can sequence them to produce a summarised version of the book in their own booklet. This activity helps children to understand the logic behind the sequence of events in a book in addition to discriminating major plot points from lesser incidents. These booklets can be used to extend the children's own writing, or the children can find and copy language patterns from the original book.

Adapting the story

Children can begin to incorporate their own ideas when adapting stories told in *Cambridge Reading* books. They might recast a story and tell it from a different point of view; they might try to transform a book into a play or puppet show; they might take an idea from the book and develop it to tell their own story. All these ideas are valid developments from the discussion which accompanies the reading of a good book. They all develop the children's reading and writing and, above all, make them feel involved in literacy.

Using the software

The disk of clip art, produced by SEMERC, contains line drawings of some of the characters from the Towards Independence books. Children can be encouraged to select images from the disk and to combine them with a simple word processing program to make pages or books on the computer. These can either be printed out to become part of the class library, or they can become part of a disk-based library of 'computer books'.

Bookmaking is a good vehicle for developing social skills and integrating the children who are less secure in their reading. The co-operation needed to develop an idea into a fully illustrated, 'published' book demands a range of skills that can be drawn from a pre-selected group of children.

Some books lend themselves much better to adaptation by children than others, and you should use your judgement to determine which books the children in your class could best adapt or retell. All the books which children produce should be read. Potential audiences include you, other children, their parents and children in other classes. There are many books available to teachers suggesting different ways of folding, cutting and stapling paper to make different books for different purposes.

Phonics for Reading

This is a resource book of teacher-led activities and worksheets which build on the phonic skills and knowledge developed in the earlier phases. The activities help children to progress beyond 'sounding out' unfamiliar words by teaching them to identify some of the most common and consistent letter strings that they will encounter in reading.

3

Language study

Language study

Language study forms an integral part of learning to read during the Towards Independence phase. Particular provision for language study at this phase includes:

- the worksheets for each book (to be found in part 2 of this teacher's book);
- the additional open-ended worksheets in this section;
- linking reading and writing through bookmaking (see pp. 30–33);
- *Phonics for Reading* – a book of photocopiable worksheets to develop spelling patterns from existing phonic knowledge (see p. 33).

Worksheets in part 2

As children become more proficient readers they can begin to devote some attention to the structure of the texts which they read and to understand issues such as:

- how the order of words within a sentence affects the meaning;
- how much a story can be enriched through the careful choice of vocabulary;
- how a story is structured and paced to retain the reader's understanding and attention;
- how punctuation and typography can be used to direct the reader's attention to important information;
- how a variety of conjunctions can be used to express different relationships between adjacent sentences.

Many of the worksheets in part 2 help to develop children's appreciation of the structure of texts through activities such as:

- sequencing and bookmaking;
- ranking plot points in order of importance;
- vocabulary extension;
- cloze procedures relating to particular parts of speech;
- comprehension activities;
- writing personal stories within a given framework.

Additional open-ended record sheets

At this phase children can also be introduced more explicitly to some of the main features of story. These include characterisation, structure, plot, mood and the way language is used to achieve particular effects.

- Characterisation – for example, a character's attributes, strengths and weaknesses; how characters relate to each other and to the reader.
- Structure – the underlying form of the story which both anticipates and satisfies the reader's expectations.
- Plot – the main events in the story and how they are linked.
- Mood – the feelings evoked by the story.
- Language use – how sentence construction and variety, and choice of vocabulary, together achieve a range of different effects by affecting the level of fluency, the tone and the degree of formality.

Some more open-ended and general photocopiable record sheets follow in this section to help you to teach about these fundamental aspects of story. They can be used or adapted for any book a child is reading or has read. The first, the Teacher/Pupil Interview Record, is for you to complete. It is followed by ten record sheets for the child to fill in:

1. Comments on books read
2. Types of stories
3. General book review
4. Looking at a character
5. Story beginnings
6. Story structure: sequence of events
7. Story structure: problem solving
8. Scene changes
9. Mood changes
10. The word collector.

Notes for language study record sheets

Teacher/Pupil Interview Record

Unlike the reading records included in section 5, this interview record focuses on the children's oral performance in responding to a book. It allows you to record how they use spoken language to:

- give reasons why the book was chosen;
- retell the story, focusing on language, sequence of events and the needs of the audience;
- demonstrate understanding of the book;
- express attitudes to reading

It is suggested that the child chooses the book. You will need to indicate whether the child already knows the book (familiar) or not (unfamiliar) as this will affect performance. A book that is familiar to the child will probably help to reveal more about their spoken language skills.

A rating scale of 1–3 can be used in the boxes: 3 indicates a very good performance, 2 a fairly good performance and 1 that the performance is weak.

1. Comments on books read

This record sheet has a dual purpose. It can either be cut into four sections, enabling four children to record their comments and ratings on a book individually, or it can be used by only one child to begin to keep a cumulative record of what they are reading. For either purpose it is helpful to discuss rating ideas, which may include a smiley/frowning face, numbers on a scale of 1 to 3 or single words.

2. Types of stories

This record sheet is designed to help children to begin to think about the four different story genres used in **Cambridge Reading**, which also feature in their wider reading. It should only be used towards the end of the year, when you can be sure that the children have read several of the titles in each genre.

The record sheet is best used in groups or with most of the class at the same time. It gives you an opportunity to *teach* about genres. For each box on the sheet, you will need to remind the children of the set of books referred to and to encourage some of them to retell one or two stories from the books in the set. As the lesson proceeds, you will need to explain concepts such as 'contemporary', 'present', 'real-life', 'events', 'retold' and 'special memories' to make sure that the activity is understood. Each group of boxes has one attribute which is not correct, so the children

need to check in the books before ticking or crossing the boxes. (This part of the activity may be better done in pairs to encourage discussion.)

You may find that this particular activity is best done over several sessions.

The last box asks for 'a memory that would make a good story'. The appropriate response in the box would begin with something like, 'Yes, I remember when I …', and consist of one or two sentences that act as a springboard for personal storytelling, story writing and bookmaking.

3. General book review

This is a general book review record sheet that concentrates on three aspects of the child's response to a book:

- an overall evaluation
- a favourite part
- a favourite character.

The boxes could be used either for writing, or for drawing and adding a caption.

4. Looking at a character

Talk with the children about some of the characters in a book and then ask which they find most interesting, attractive or thought-provoking. Record on a piece of paper some of the words you and the children use to describe the characters, and make sure that the children can see the paper when they are completing the record sheet. Emphasise during the discussion that most characters have weak points as well as strengths.

5. Story beginnings

This record sheet – which need only be used once by each child – helps you to teach about effective story beginnings and helps the children to reflect on this important aspect of a story.

Once the children have chosen their own story beginning, ask them to say why they chose it before they copy it out. If the record sheet is to be completed in a group, the children can discuss each other's choices before they complete it.

6. Story structure: sequence of events

This is best introduced in a group, using the same story. Discuss with the children what happens to start the story moving, what the three most important events in the plot are (there may be more but you will have to be selective) and how the story ends. For the middle three boxes you can ask the children to say what they think are the most important events and record them on the record sheet.

The record sheet can be used again by individual children, as appropriate, in response to other stories.

Less able writers can draw events in some of the boxes.

7. Story structure: problem solving

Many stories are structured around a problem and its solution. Select a story with a clear problem and discuss the nature of the problem with the children. An example is *Don't Be Late!* Focus on how the author chose to solve the problem. (Are there any alternative solutions?) The children are then ready to fill in the record sheet.

8. Scene changes

This record sheet focuses on how the structure of a story is often reflected in the way it changes scenes. Read *The Slippery Planet* with the children and then ask them to check that the flow chart on the record sheet is accurate as a record of scene changes. (Some scene changes are not shown – see if the children can spot and explain this.) The children can then make their own flow charts showing scene changes in a book they already know well. Some children will prefer not to write sentences; nouns (e.g. 'planet', 'spaceship') will do.

9. Mood changes

As a plot twists and turns, the mood both of the story and the reader often changes too. This record sheet helps the children to become aware of feelings within the story and of their reaction to them. Share a book with a group, then ask the children to identify some examples of different moods. Write their ideas on a piece of paper. When the children fill in the sheet they should describe the mood in the flash and write about it in the larger shape.

10. The word collector

This record sheet focuses on words the children find interesting and unfamiliar in their books. To introduce the record sheet, complete worksheet 1 from *The Cape of Rushes*. The words at the top of the record sheet are taken from that worksheet. Read these words aloud and in the context of the sentences from the book.

The children should then look through a book which they have recently read and choose some words which they find interesting and unfamiliar to write in the spaces provided. Using the context from the book, they should then try to define the word themselves, or suggest a synonym, before looking it up in a dictionary or thesaurus.

Some children may enjoy keeping a copy of this record sheet near them whenever they read so they can note down interesting words and think about their meaning.

Teacher/Pupil Interview Record

Name ———————————— Teacher ———————————— Date ————————————

Title	Book chosen by	Familiar/unfamiliar
Author	Reason for choosing	
Stage		

Retold the story to ————————————————————————————,

☐ making good use of the pictures

☐ using some words and phrases in the text

☐ sequencing correctly

☐ including all/most important events/points

☐ using expression, taking audience needs into account

☐ showing enthusiasm and pleasure

Notes on a discussion of the text.

For the immediate future we agreed

Teacher/Pupil Interview Record

Title Spike & the Concert	Book chosen by Jo	Familiar/~~unfamiliar~~
Author June Crebbin Stage T.1. <u>C</u>	Reason for choosing "This story makes me laugh. I wish I had a dog like spike."	

Retold the story to __teacher in 1-1 context__ ,

☑ making good use of the pictures

☐ using some words and phrases in the text

☑ sequencing correctly

☑ including ~~all~~/most important events/points

☐ using expression, taking audience needs into account

☑ showing enthusiasm and pleasure

Notes on a discussion of the text.

Retelling used a lot of reference to the pictures — "and then this girl went over here" — but wasn't in 'book language'.

Story understood and enjoyed, evoking anecdotes from own life. Some difficulty distinguishing the main points from the trivia.

For the immediate future we agreed to have more of these interviews — we both enjoyed it! Responsibility devolved to Jo to choose another book sometime soon and to ask for a reading interview.
Next time we'll think more about 'book language'.

Name _____   Date _____

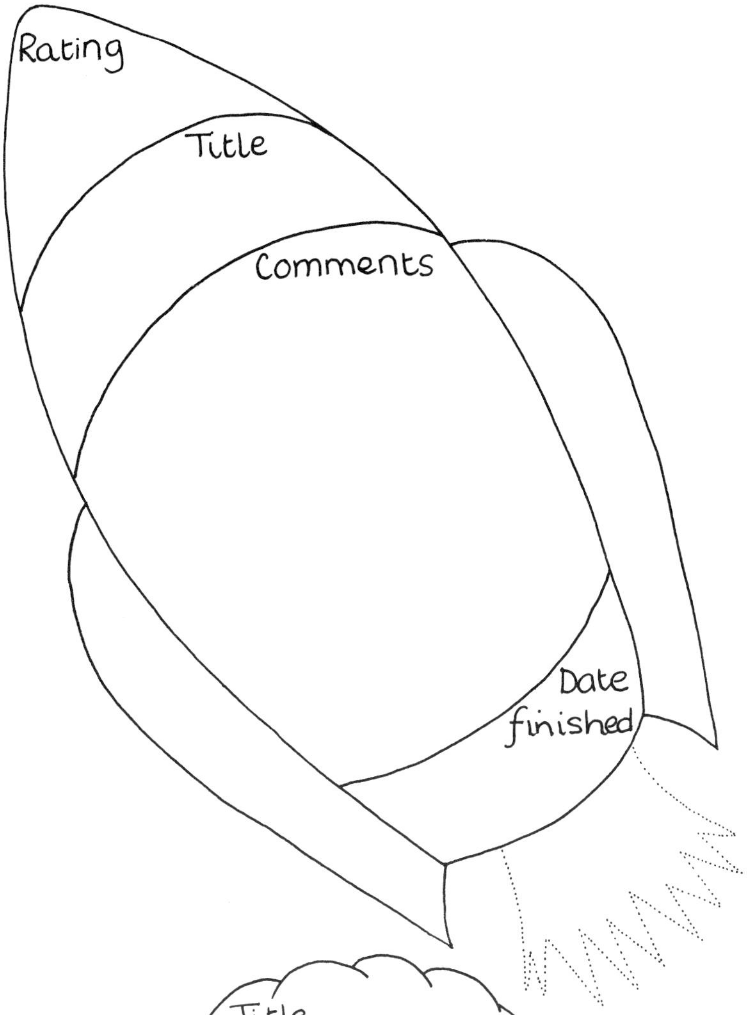

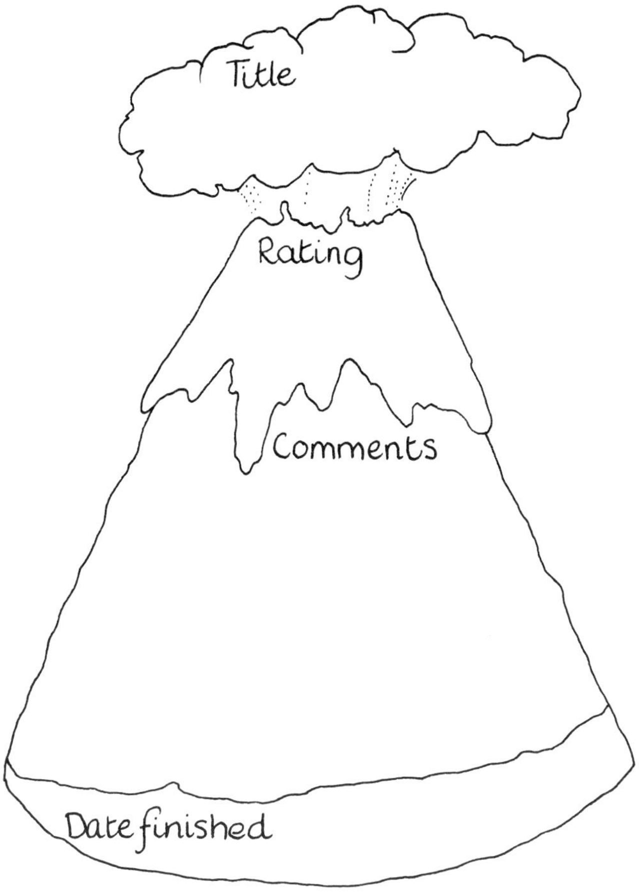

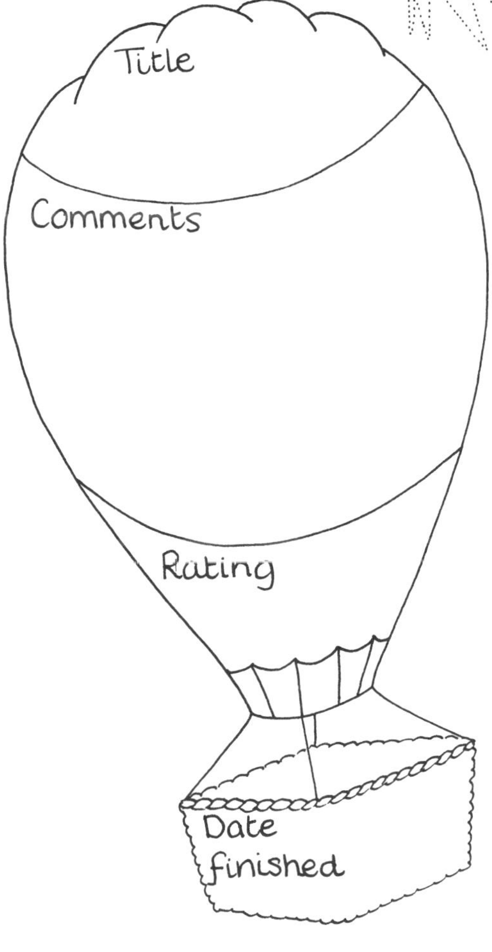

Rating

Title

Comments

Date finished

Title

Rating

Comments

Date finished

Title

Comments

Rating

Date finished

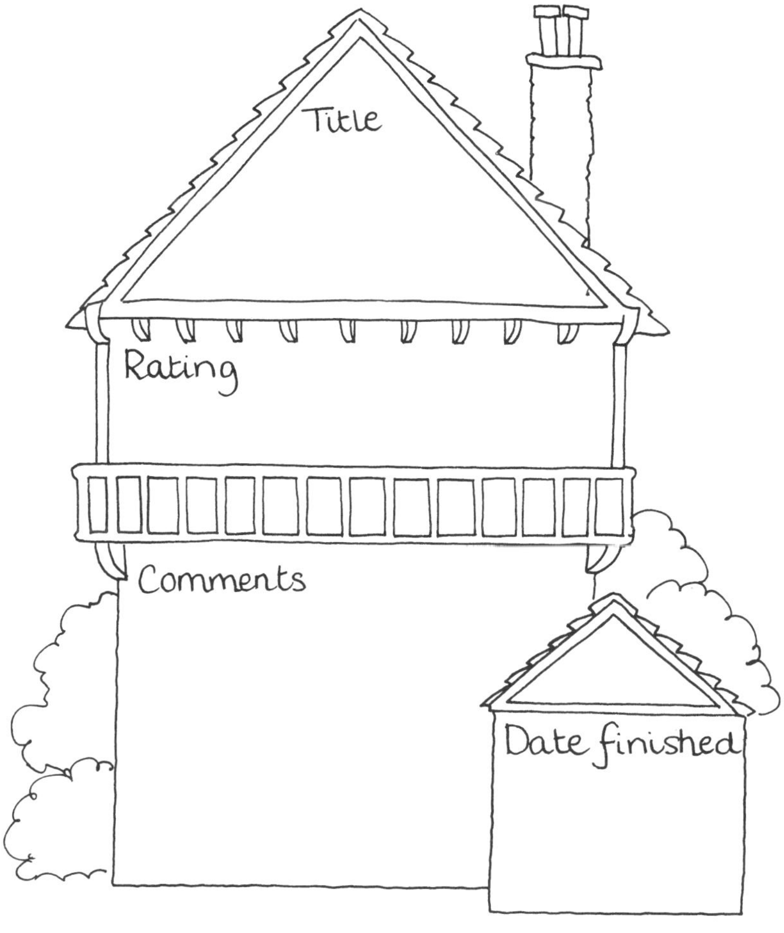

Title

Rating

Comments

Date finished

Language study 1: Comments on books read   41

Name _____ Date _____

Tick the boxes which are right.

Contemporary stories by June Crebbin ☐ happen in the present ☐ could happen in real life ☐ are always funny	Which story did you like best? _____ Why did you like it?
Fantasy stories by Rosemary Hayes ☐ have events which couldn't happen in real life ☐ always have magic spells ☐ often have invented places	Which story was the most exciting? _____ What made it exciting?
Traditional tales ☐ are retold by the authors ☐ are usually very old ☐ often have magic or mystery ☐ always have animals in them	Which story would be the best one to read to your class? _____ Why?
Stories of childhood by Richard Brown ☐ are about real-life events ☐ happened many years ago ☐ are retold by the author ☐ are special memories ☐ the person who tells the story is always 'I'	Have you got a memory that would make a good story?

Name _____   Date _____

Title _____

Author _____   Illustrator _____

I thought this book was

because

My favourite part was

The character I liked best was

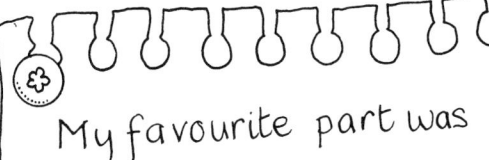

You can find it on page(s)

Name _____ Date _____

Title _____ Author _____

Draw and name the character that most interests you.

Name

Which words best describe this character?

This character's good points.

This character's weak points.

If you could step into the story and meet this character, what would you ask them?

What makes these good story beginnings?

The Pyjama Party
In two weeks' time Emma would be eight.
"Time to make plans," said Mum. "Plans for a party."
    "Oh good," said Emma. "What kind of party?"

The Weather Drum
Long, long ago, there was a terrible storm.
First, a strong wind began to blow.
Then lightning and thunder boomed and flashed across the sky.

I think this is a good story beginning because

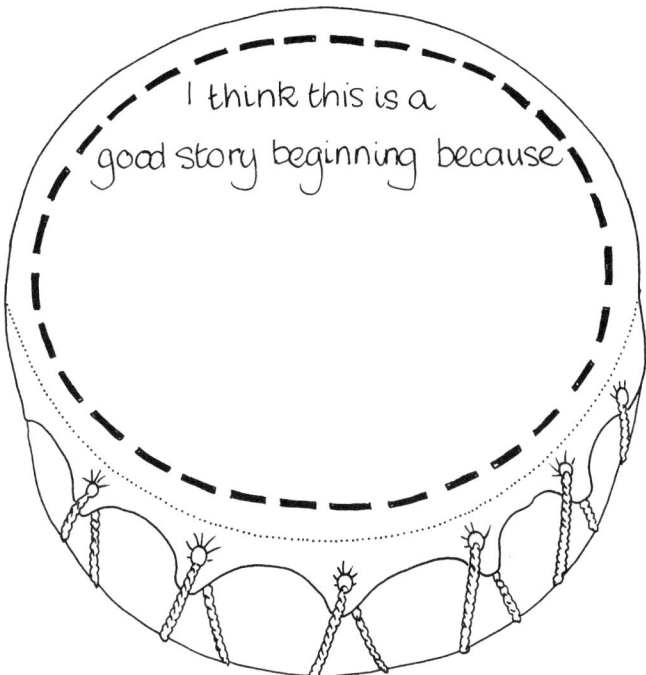

I think this is a good story beginning because

Choose a story beginning that you like. Copy it here.

Title and author

The story began

The first important event was

Then

After that

The story ended when

CAMBRIDGE
READING

Title and author

Draw who had the problem

Write what the problem was

How was the problem solved?

Name _____ Date _____

The story in *The Slippery Planet* has many changes of scene.

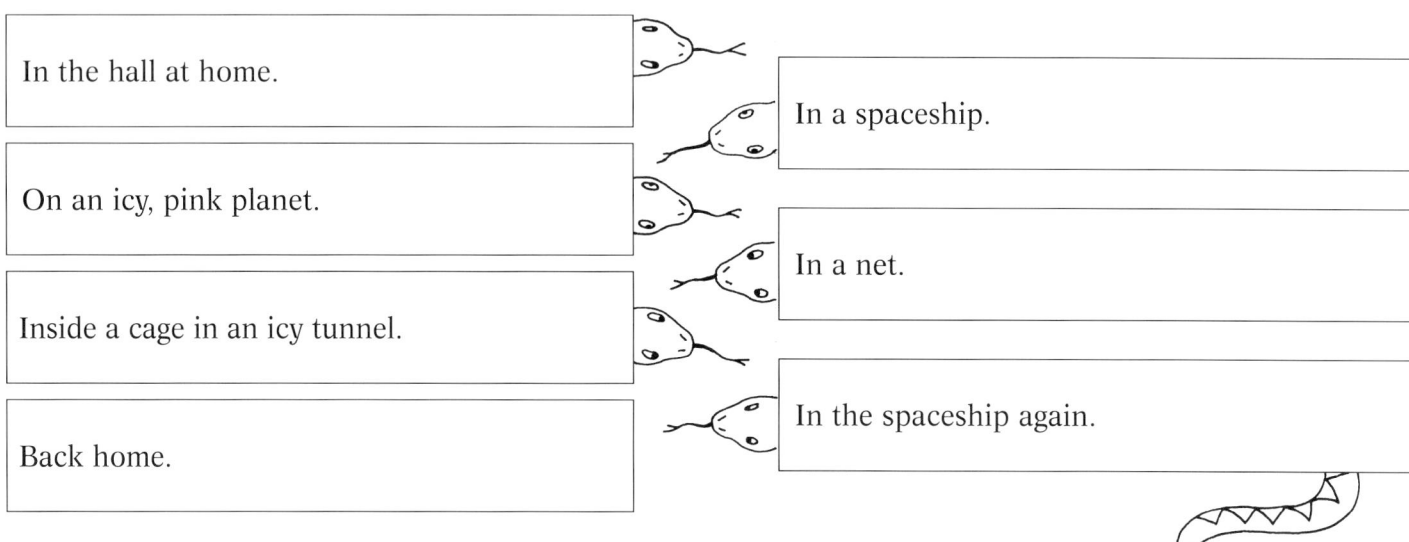

In the hall at home.	
On an icy, pink planet.	In a spaceship.
Inside a cage in an icy tunnel.	In a net.
Back home.	In the spaceship again.

Choose a story you like. Write in the boxes all the different scene changes you can find in it.

Title _____ Author _____

© CUP 1996.

Name _____ Date _____

Title _____ Author _____

In a good story, the mood often changes.
What are the moods in this story?

Write the mood in the ⬚.
Write about that bit of the story.

You can use some of these words to
give you ideas.

silly   frightening

exciting   fun   clever

mysterious   sad

happy   gentle

Word collectors like to collect interesting words.

These words are taken from page 8 of *The Cape of Rushes*.

fine   fringed   gathered

nimble   bedraggled   dainty

Look through some books that you have read and pick out some words that you find interesting.

Try to guess what they mean, then look them up in a dictionary.

The word is...	I think it means...	The dictionary says...

4

Home–school links

The importance of home reading

Education is a partnership between home and school. Making the most of this partnership is extremely important for the children's progress through school.

Most parents like to feel that they are directly involved with their children's education and, since they generally regard reading as a high priority, they want to be involved with helping their children to learn to read. There are many advantages in having parental support for your teaching:

- Most parents have more time than the teacher has to read with their children and to talk about books they are reading.

- If children learn to associate books with special, individual time with a parent, they are more likely to be positive about books and to look forward to their reading time.

- At home, most children are not in competition with their peers, so they can read at their own pace.

- Parents are best placed to know about their children's previous experience and prior knowledge. They can build on this knowledge to help children create a context for the books they read.

- Most parents are enthusiastic about their children's progress and will talk about it with friends and relatives. This helps children to feel positive about reading.

Communicating with parents

To help you to communicate with parents and to explain how best they can help their children to learn to read with *Cambridge Reading*, this section includes:

- a letter to send to parents (for photocopying or adapting) which outlines briefly which phase their child is reading at and gives some general ideas for reading at home (space has been left for your school's letterhead);

- a photocopiable leaflet for parents, offering advice and suggestions on how to make home reading enjoyable and successful;

- a Home Reading Record, which shows parents that you value their opinion on their child's reading habits.

All of these communications are probably best introduced during meetings with parents.

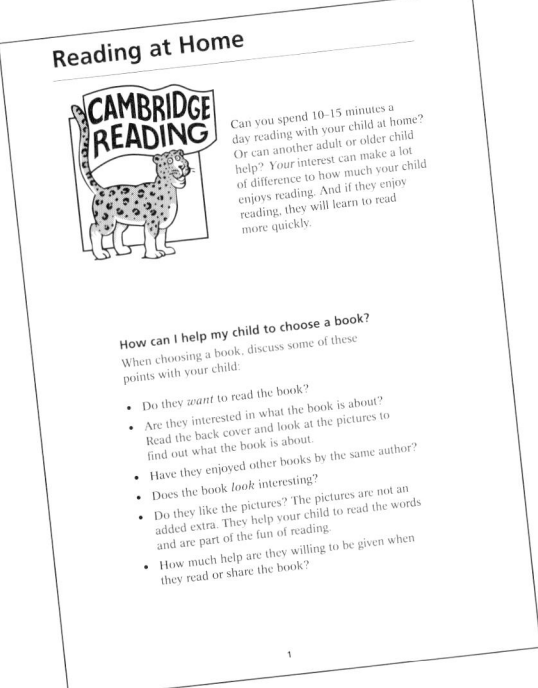

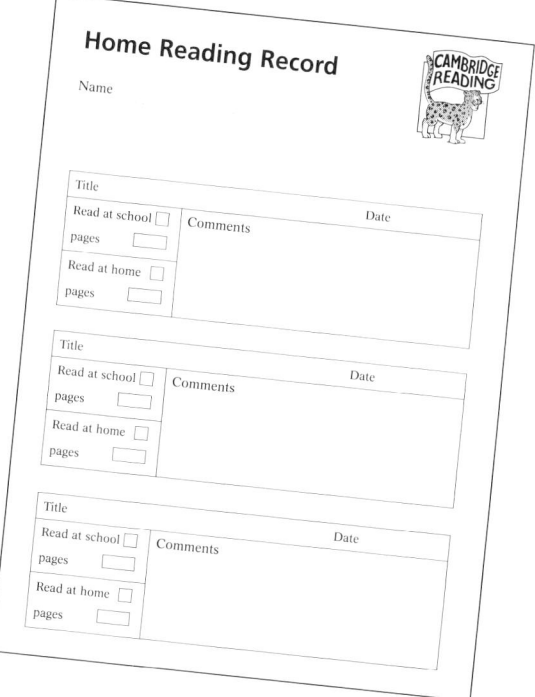

Dear

Your child has enjoyed many of the books in the first two phases of our main reading scheme, **Cambridge Reading** and is now ready to move on to the third phase of the scheme, which is called Towards Independence.

As the name of the phase implies, your child will be reading the books they bring home with increasing independence, and will need much less help than before; but you can continue to support their progress by hearing them read and by talking about the book together. You will find more detailed advice about how to help your child at home in our Reading at Home leaflet.

Although your child will be reading more to themselves at this stage, they will need your support and interest, to encourage them to become a skilled and enthusiastic reader.

We would like you to continue to let us know about how your child is responding to books and reading at home by using our Home Reading Record. If you have any concerns about your child's progress you can arrange a time to talk these over.

We very much value the support you give to our home–school reading partnership, and we feel sure that the help your child receives at home will support their success at school.

Happy reading!

Reading at Home

Can you spend 10–15 minutes a day reading with your child at home? Or can another adult or older child help? *Your* interest can make a lot of difference to how much your child enjoys reading. And if they enjoy reading, they will learn to read more quickly.

How can I help my child to choose a book?

When choosing a book, discuss some of these points with your child:

- Do they *want* to read the book?
- Are they interested in what the book is about? Read the back cover and look at the pictures to find out what the book is about.
- Have they enjoyed other books by the same author?
- Does the book *look* interesting?
- Do they like the pictures? The pictures are not an added extra. They help your child to read the words and are part of the fun of reading.
- How much help are they willing to be given when they read or share the book?

When is the best time for reading at home?

- Any time when you can both settle down and relax for 10–15 minutes.
- Any time when you are not going to be interrupted.
- Any time when neither you nor your child is too tired.
- Any time when your child isn't missing a favourite TV programme!

How long should your reading time last?

- No more than about 10–15 minutes for most children. You should always stop before your child gets restless.
- Frequent, short periods spent reading are better than one long session.

The most important thing is that you and your child should *enjoy* your reading time. Praise their efforts and try to end on a positive, successful note.

If you need more help, or if you have any worries about your child's reading, please talk to their class teacher about your concerns.

What should I do if my child keeps choosing a book that is too easy?

Children are *not* wasting their time when they read easy or familiar books as all reading practice is valuable. But you can help them to feel more confident about moving on to more difficult books. Here are some suggestions:

- Praise them when they read an easy book with feeling and understanding.

- Start your reading time with a new book and end with an old favourite.

- Help them to choose a more difficult book and offer to read it aloud with them if they wish.

What should I do if my child chooses a book that is too difficult?

- Ask if they would like you to read the book to them first. It isn't cheating! While your child is listening, they are getting to know the book and are remembering words and phrases.

- Read aloud at the same time as your child, letting them set the pace. If they hesitate over a word, just keep on reading quietly. The child will soon join in again.

- Take turns to read pages.

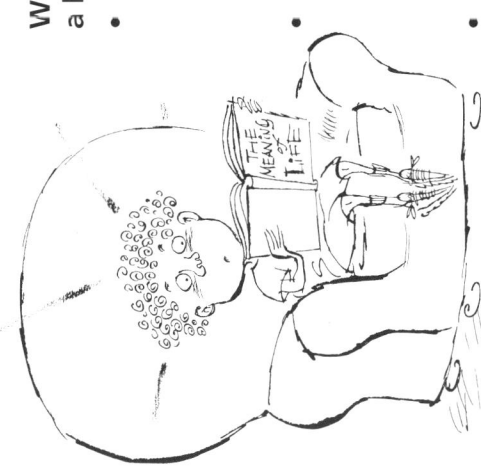

What is the best way to get started?

Talk to your child about the book before you start reading.

- If the book is **familiar**, ask questions that will help your child give *their* opinion about what happens in the book. There is a list of helpful questions on page 3 of this leaflet.

- If the book is **unfamiliar**, encourage your child to guess what the book may be about. There are lots of clues they can use: the title, the description of the book on the cover, the pictures.

2

What should I do if my child gets stuck on a word?

Try to *vary* the help you give your child. This will encourage them to learn new ways of coping when they get stuck. Here are some suggestions:

- Quietly say the missing word so that the flow of the sentence is not broken.

- Encourage them to refer to the picture.

- Read the first sound or syllable of the word to them.

- Read the whole sentence, missing out the word.

How can we best talk about the book afterwards?

This will depend on your child's interests and the book. Questions that simply test how many details a child has remembered ('What was the dog's name?' or 'How many children were there in the story?') are unlikely to interest them much.

Here are some suggestions of questions that should involve your child more:

- What is their favourite moment?

- What parts did they like best?

- Which character would they like to have been? Why?

- Have they ever felt the same way as one of the characters?

- Has something similar ever happened to them?

- Do they remember the time when ...?

- What do they think would have happened if ...?

- *Why* do they think ...?

- What else could have happened after ...?

- What did they think about the ending?

3

Notes for the Home Reading Record

A photocopiable Home Reading Record is provided to help you keep track of children's reading at home and to share observations and information about their reading progress with their parents/guardians. It is intended that parents/guardians should use the Home Reading Record in conjunction with the Reading at Home leaflet.

To make the record, the two photocopiable masters should be copied back-to-back and folded down the middle.

The title of each book that the child takes home should be entered in the appropriate box.

If the child has read some of the book at school, the page numbers can be written in the space provided. Pages read at home can also be recorded.

Comments

This box has at least three applications:

- The teacher may want to write a message to the child's parent/guardian; for example, the page numbers you want the child to read at home or why this book has been chosen.

- The child's parent/guardian can record a brief statement about how the reading went and/or what they thought of the book. This may include vocabulary difficulties, reading stamina, whether the book was too challenging and so on.

- The child can at times be encouraged to write their own comments about the book.

Title	Spike and the Comet		Date 10/11
Read at school ✓	Comments	Read well but without	
pages 2-14	much expression. KC.		
Read at home ✓	Used different voices for different		
pages 2-14	people speaking. CB		

Home Reading Record

Name

Title		Date
Read at school ☐	Comments	
pages ☐		
Read at home ☐		
pages ☐		

Title		Date
Read at school ☐	Comments	
pages ☐		
Read at home ☐		
pages ☐		

Title		Date
Read at school ☐	Comments	
pages ☐		
Read at home ☐		
pages ☐		

Title		Date
Read at school ☐	Comments	
pages ☐		
Read at home ☐		
pages ☐		

Title		Date
Read at school ☐	Comments	
pages ☐		
Read at home ☐		
pages ☐		

Favourite books re-read:

Date

Card 1 (top row)

Title

Date

Read at school ☐

pages ☐

Read at home ☐

pages ☐

Comments

Card 2 (top row)

Title

Date

Read at school ☐

pages ☐

Read at home ☐

pages ☐

Comments

Card 3 (top row)

Title

Date

Read at school ☐

pages ☐

Read at home ☐

pages ☐

Comments

Card 4 (top row)

Title

Date

Read at school ☐

pages ☐

Read at home ☐

pages ☐

Comments

Card 5 (bottom row)

Title

Date

Read at school ☐

pages ☐

Read at home ☐

pages ☐

Comments

Card 6 (bottom row)

Title

Date

Read at school ☐

pages ☐

Read at home ☐

pages ☐

Comments

Card 7 (bottom row)

Title

Date

Read at school ☐

pages ☐

Read at home ☐

pages ☐

Comments

Card 8 (bottom row)

Title

Date

Read at school ☐

pages ☐

Read at home ☐

pages ☐

Comments

Record-keeping and assessment

Listening skills

Always sits quietly but comprehension isn't generally very good on 1st hearing. Can usually answer simple questions on 2nd hearing. Seems to enjoy being read to.

Sharing books in pairs and groups

Prefers to let someone else do the reading. Reluctant even to shared read in group. Once the story is understood will generally chat happily about it.

Reading aloud

Prefers being read to! Reluctant to attempt new stories, even after sharing. Reading still very mechanical and staccato. Takes several re-readings before any degree of fluency is reached. Punctuation disregarded.

Decoding skills and strategies

Still needs a lot of picture support. Beginning to use cvc and ccv phonic cues to guide a guess but phonic knowledge still inadequate. Relies heavily on known sight words to provide the framework for guessing - often with success.

Response and comprehension

Sharing a book is essential before any degree of comprehension is achieved. Responses are often limited by poor vocabulary, but generally willing to chat about events in the book.

Attitudes to reading

Still enjoys everything about reading except reading! Needs more experience of books which are manageable to bolster confidence & reinforce comprehension.

Knowledge about books and other media

Limited. Doesn't read by choice. Asks others to read for him.

Recording and assessing reading development

All teachers of children who are learning to read recognise the importance of keeping records of a child's reading development. The records range in form from a teacher's individual notes to internal records, reports and national test results.

Keeping records of progress in reading allows you to be sure:

- that your children are learning at a satisfactory rate;
- that you identify children who are not making the progress expected;
- that your teaching is effective;
- that you are carrying out school policy;
- that the resources you use are appropriate;
- that areas of particular need are highlighted;
- that other interested parties can be kept informed of the child's progress.

Records and assessment for reading tend to fall into three categories:

- quantitative, e.g. a list of the books a child has shared, read and responded to, categorised into levels of difficulty;
- formative, e.g. a record of how a child responds to a particular text;
- summative, e.g. a summary of what a child has achieved over a period of time, noting reading behaviour which has become secure.

A summary of the Reading Records

Record 1: books read and worksheets completed

This record sheet, which is appropriate for both individual children and groups, enables you to keep track of books read and worksheets completed using a very simple format.

Record 2: hearing a child read

This helps you to make a structured observation of a child's strengths and strategies when reading and responding to a particular text.

Record 3: reading behaviour

This allows you to record, over time, aspects of the child's reading development, including attitudes, concepts, strategies and responses.

Record 4: a summary of reading behaviour

Many teachers prefer record formats which allow space to record written comments.

This is an open-ended record to allow for individual observation of a child's strengths and strategies.

Children's own reading records

Children can make records of their own reading by using a book-review sheet (provided on p. 71) or a bookmark (provided on p. 72).

Other records

A Home Reading Record can be found on pages 57–58. Record sheets for language skills can be found on pages 39–50.

Reading Record 1 Books read and worksheets completed

R = Reading development

P = Personal response

☐ = non-fiction titles

Towards Independence A

Title	R	P
Cutting and Sticking	R	P
Parrot Talk	R	P
Strawberry Picking	R	P
In the Mirror	R	P
The Big Shrink	R	P
Marvel Paws	R	P
The Grabbing Bird	R	P
The Treasure Cave	R	P
Nonsense!	R	P
Dancing to the River	R	P
Animal Communication	R	P
How the Animals Got Their Tails	R	P
Camouflage	R	P
Rabbit's Tail	R	P
Codes and Signals	R	P

Towards Independence B

Title	R	P
Ben's Amazing Birthday	R	P
The Dog Show	R	P
Dad's Promise	R	P
The Pyjama Party	R	P
Tulips for Dad	R	P
The Special Cake	R	P
The Haystack	R	P
Jumble Power	R	P
A Corner of Magic	R	P
The Magic Sword	R	P
A Lick of the Spoon	R	P
The Peace Ring	R	P
Knickerbocker Number Nine	R	P
The Lord Mount Dragon	R	P
A Book of Hours	R	P
The Weather Drum	R	P
Noah's Ark	R	P
Volcano Woman	R	P
The Tomb of Nebamun	R	P

Towards Independence C

Title	R	P
A Shoot of Corn	R	P
A Cat for Keeps	R	P
Snow in the Kitchen	R	P
Don't Be Late!	R	P
The Watch by the Sea	R	P
Spike and the Concert	R	P
A Mosquito in the Cabin	R	P
Mr Mulch's Magic Mixtures	R	P
Out and About	R	P
The Amazing Mr Mulch	R	P
Welcome Night	R	P
The Slippery Planet	R	P
Coral Reef	R	P
Coyote Girl	R	P
Desert	R	P
The Cape of Rushes	R	P
Rainforest	R	P
The Most Beautiful Child	R	P

Cambridge Reading Teacher's Book 3 © Cambridge University Press 1996.

Notes for Reading Record 1:
books read and worksheets completed

The following is a suggested recording system that you could use to keep track of the books read and shared, and worksheets completed, by individual children. This recording system can also be used to keep track of small reading groups, or pairs of children working together.

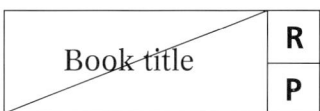 The book has been read by the child (with some prompting, as appropriate).

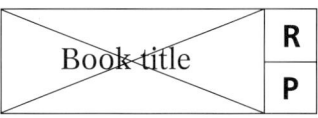 The book has been shared in a group or pair.

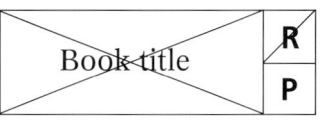 The child has successfully completed the reading development worksheet for this book.

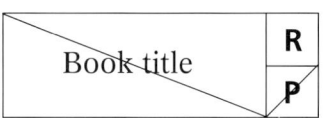 The child has successfully completed the personal response worksheet for this book.

Reading Record 2 Hearing a child read

Name ....

Year ....

Teacher ....

Date ....

Title ....

Phase .... Stage ....

Pages heard ....

☐ Story
☐ Poetry
☐ Non-fiction

Was the child
☐ new to the book *or*
☐ familiar with the book?

Reading aloud	Recall

Unknown words decoded

Using context cues	Using picture cues	Using grammatical cues (syntax)	Using phonic and spelling cues

Common words not recognised on sight

Specific problems	The next steps

Notes for Reading Record 2:
hearing a child read

This record can be used as frequently as you think is necessary to record how a child is responding to a book which is at their instructional level. It should help you to record:

- the child's skills in reading aloud;
- the child's ability to recall the main events of the text (comprehension);
- unknown words that the child successfully decodes and the cueing strategies used;
- the sight words the child needs to learn;

- specific problems that need attention;
- the next steps in the child's reading path.

It is important to remember that different texts may give different results. A child is likely to respond in different ways to information books, books of poems and story-books. And whether a child finds a book easy or challenging may well depend upon how familiar they are with it. It makes sense, then, to use this observational record several times a year, using different kinds of books to gain a fuller picture of the child's responses.

Reading Record 2 Hearing a child read

Name Peter

Year 2

Teacher Mrs Ruttle

Date July '96

Title How the Animals Got Their Tails

Phase Towards Ind.　　Stage A

Pages heard All

☑ Story　　*Was the child*
☐ Poetry　　☐ new to the book *or*
☐ Non-fiction　　☑ familiar with the book?

Reading aloud
Even with a familiar book, reading is hesitant. Appears to be reading one word at a time without scanning ahead. No regard to punctuation.

Recall
The book was chosen because it is familiar. It took two or three readings for true understanding but now general recall and comprehension are good.
Still can't scan the pages to isolate details in the text.
Enjoys talking about books.

Unknown words decoded

Using context cues	Using picture cues	Using grammatical cues (syntax)	Using phonic and spelling cues
Not much in evidence. eg suggested 'boxes' for 'bosses' on p 3.	Still needs a lot of support from pictures.	Miscues generally grammatically appropriate.	Beginning to use initial blends + vowel but can't read beyond first syllable.

Common words not recognised on sight
Basic sight words generally secure.

Specific problems
1) phonic skills need reinforcement
2) comprehension not always secure
3) general vocabulary + sentence structure need work.

The next steps
Try some Bridging books to focus on 1) and 2)
Find time to talk about books!

Reading Record 3 A checklist of reading behaviour

Name ....

Y2/P3 teacher ....

Y3/P4 teacher ....

Reading aloud	Decoding skills and strategies	Response and comprehension	Attitudes to reading	Knowledge about books and other media
☐ has dispensed with finger/card marker ☐ reads familiar texts with fluency ☐ reads unfamiliar texts with some fluency ☐ fluent with unfamiliar texts ☐ uses punctuation to guide intonation ☐ uses some expression ☐ uses different voices to denote different characters ☐ paces performance ☐ uses appropriate tone of voice ☐ can give a prepared reading to an audience	*Phonics* ☐ decodes simple, phonically regular words ☐ decodes syllable by syllable decodes using: ☐ consonant blends and digraphs ☐ vowel digraphs ☐ silent letters ☐ prefixes and suffixes ☐ is over-reliant on phonic cues *Picture/context cues* ☐ makes good use of picture cues ☐ can use context and prior knowledge to predict unknown words *Syntactic cues* ☐ scans ahead ☐ re-reads sentence *Self-correcting* self-corrects using: ☐ picture cues ☐ semantic cues ☐ syntactic cues ☐ phonic cues	☐ reads for meaning by keeping overall sense of passage ☐ discusses illustrations ☐ retells story, sequencing main events in correct order ☐ expresses personal response to text ☐ repeats some points of text ☐ interprets characterisation and motive in story line ☐ evaluates a text giving reasons for opinions ☐ summarises main points of text ☐ infers and develops ideas not specifically stated ☐ distinguishes between fact and fiction ☐ comments on style of writing and vocabulary	enjoys: ☐ fiction ☐ poetry ☐ plays ☐ picture books ☐ non-fiction ☐ often opts to read when given a free choice ☐ rarely opts to read when given a free choice ☐ reads silently ☐ has favourite books and authors ☐ can choose books from a library/ bookshelf giving reasons for choice ☐ enjoys talking about books read ☐ explores a wide range of different genres ☐ reads or shares books at a variety of levels ☐ always has at least one book 'on the go'	uses: ☐ blurbs ☐ contents pages ☐ indexes ☐ glossaries knows alphabetical order to: ☐ 1st letter ☐ 2nd letter ☐ 3rd letter ☐ uses a dictionary effectively ☐ recognises differences between different purposes of books ☐ uses a simple library classification system including a catalogue reads: ☐ comics ☐ magazines ☐ newspapers ☐ computer software ☐ begins to recognise bias (including adverts) in printed and visual media

 Cambridge Reading Teacher's Book 3 © Cambridge University Press 1996.

Notes for Reading Record 3: a checklist of reading behaviour

The four columns in the record allow you to record different aspects of a child's reading development, including reading aloud, decoding, response and comprehension, attitudes, and knowledge about books and other media. The record is designed to be used for as long as it proves useful. You can tick the items on the sheet to indicate the child's knowledge, behaviour and attitudes which you consider to be secure. Additionally, you can use a highlighter pen over items in the record, using a different colour pen for each school year.

Reading aloud

The skill of reading aloud has many different aspects, including fluency, expression, tone and pace. This column allows you to record the skills the child displays when reading aloud to you and to other audiences.

☑ has dispensed with finger/card marker

☑ reads familiar texts with fluency

☐ reads unfamiliar texts with some

Decoding skills and strategies

Proficient readers are able to use a wide range of decoding strategies. This column enables you to record the decoding strategies a child deploys. It should also alert you to a child who is reliant upon one particular area for too long.

Phonics

☑ decodes simple, phonically regular words

☑ decodes syllable by syllable

Picture/context cues

☑ makes good use of picture cues

☐ can use context and prior knowledge to predict unknown

Self-correcting

self-corrects using:
☑ picture cues
☐ semantic cues
☐ syntactic cues
☐ phonic cues

Response and comprehension

Once a child has finished reading a passage, they should sometimes recall, review, comment on and evaluate the text to show that they have understood it fully. This column allows you to record what the child is able to do while responding to a text and to record the level of their comprehension skills.

☑ discusses illustrations

☑ retells story, sequencing main events in correct order

☑ expresses personal response to text

Attitudes to reading

Attitude and motivation will greatly affect the child's success at reading. This column allows you to record different reading behaviours which indicate a child's attitude to reading.

enjoys:
☐ fiction
☑ poetry
☐ plays
☑ picture books
☐ non-fiction

☐ often opts to read when given a free choice

☑ rarely opts to read when given a free choice

☑ reads silently

Knowledge about books and other media

This column allows you to record the child's skill in using reference materials and in locating and retrieving information, and their experience of other printed media.

uses:
☐ blurbs
☑ contents pages
☑ indexes
☐ glossaries

knows alphabetical order to:
☑ 1st letter
☐ 2nd letter
☐ 3rd letter

Reading Record 4 A summary of reading behaviour

Name ....

Year ....

Teacher ....

Date ....

Listening skills	Sharing books in pairs and groups

Reading aloud

Decoding skills and strategies

Response and comprehension

Attitudes to reading	Knowledge about books and other media

Cambridge Reading Teacher's Book 3 © Cambridge University Press 1996.

Notes for Reading Record 4:
a summary of reading behaviour

Many teachers prefer record formats which allow them space to record written comments. Reading Record 4 provides a framework to allow for individual observation. It can be used as frequently as the need arises, but two or three times a year may be adequate for most children.

Listening skills

You might wish to record here how attentively the child listens to texts aloud and how much they draw upon their memory of the text in a subsequent shared reading session.

> **Listening skills**
> Always sits quietly, but comprehension isn't generally very good on 1st hearing. Can usually answer simple questions on 2nd hearing.
> Seems to enjoy being read to.

Sharing books in pairs and groups

Since sharing books in pairs and groups is such an important part of a child's early reading experience, it is worth recording here the child's general behaviour and attitude to this form of reading. For example, does the child join in? Are they comfortable sharing with another child?

> **Sharing books in pairs and groups**
> Prefers to let someone else do the reading. Reluctant even to choral read in group.
> Once the story is understood, will generally chat happily about it.

Reading aloud

Here, you may wish to record:

- fluency;
- expression;
- attention to punctuation;
- pace and pause;
- finger–line/finger–word match;
- confidence;
- stamina;
- teaching points.

> **Reading aloud**
> Prefers being read to! Reluctant to attempt new stories, even after sharing. Reading still very mechanical and staccato. Takes several re-readings before any degree of fluency is reached. Punctuation disregarded.

Decoding skills and strategies

Here, you may wish to record:

- which strategies the child uses to decode unknown words;
- if the child relies too heavily on one or two strategies;
- teaching points.

> **Decoding skills and strategies**
> Still needs a lot of picture support.
> Beginning to use CVC and CCV phonic cues to guide a guess, but phonic knowledge still inadequate.
> Relies heavily on known sight words to provide the framework for guessing- often with success.

Response and comprehension

The most effective way of finding out if a child has understood a text is to discuss it with them, encouraging recall, comment, sequencing, opinion and the expression of preferences.

> **Response and comprehension**
> Sharing a book is essential before any degree of comprehension is achieved.
> Responses are often limited by poor vocabulary, but generally willing to chat about events in the book.

Attitudes to reading

Any progress that a child makes is largely dependent on their attitude towards reading. Is their attitude positive, confident, experimental, or is it anxious, hesitant, stilted? The latter should alert you to problems which need to be identified and tackled.

> **Attitudes to reading**
> Still enjoys everything about reading except reading!
> Needs more experience of books which are manageable to bolster confidence & reinforce comprehension.

Knowledge about books and other media

As children become more proficient readers they need to learn how to find information about the books they read. This includes making use of information on the cover/contents page of a book and finding books in libraries. You can also record children's referencing skills and preferred reading context.

> **Knowledge about books and other media**
> Limited. Doesn't read by choice.
> Asks others to read for him.

Name _____

Date _____

Which book did
you read?

_____

by

_____

What did you
like about this
book?

_____

_____

_____

Draw the best
part of the story.

What happened?

_____

_____

_____

Cambridge Reading Teacher's Book 3 © Cambridge University Press 1996.

This bookmark belongs to _____

What books have you read?

Which ones did you like best?

This bookmark belongs to _____

What books have you read?

Which ones did you like best?

This bookmark belongs to _____

What books have you read?

Which ones did you like best?

Notes for children's own reading records

To help children begin to reflect on and write about the books they are enjoying, two photocopiable sheets are provided. One is a book review framework which encourages the children to say what they liked about a book and what they think was the best part of it. The other is a bookmark on which the children can record the books they have shared, or read, indicating their overall response to each, for example by using a smiley face symbol. There are nine spaces for titles on the bookmark, allowing the child to record the nine titles in each set of books at the Towards Independence stage. This page can be photocopied, and each bookmark can then be cut out and stuck onto card.

This bookmark belongs to

Victoria Clare Ruttle

What books have you read?

Animals Tails 😊

Paddling to the river 😊

Rabbit Tails 😐

Weather Drum 😊

Volcano Woman 😊

Lord Mount Dragon ☀

Cape of Rushes 😟

Beautiful child 😐

Coyote Girl 😊

Which ones did you like best?

2 PART TWO:
Teacher's Pages and worksheets

Cutting and Sticking

Author June Crebbin

Illustrator Peter Kavanagh

Strand contemporary

Towards Independence: A

Other books in the strand at this stage

- Parrot Talk
- Strawberry Picking

Introducing the book

- Talk about the cover, including the title and blurb. Invite predictions about the book's contents.

After reading the book

- Discuss what things you may need when decorating. What experiences do the children have of decorating?

- Ask the children to think of times when helping at home caused trouble. Those with younger brothers and sisters could talk about the difficulties that can occur when young children try to help.

WORKSHEET 1
Reading Development

Activity *Comprehension and recall*

- Check that the children understand what 'true' and 'false' mean.

- Ask the children to write 'true' or 'false' next to statements relating to the story. It may be appropriate for some to record their answers by using 'T' or 'F'.

- Some children may need to be given the numbers of pages where the answers are to be found.

Answers 1 False (p. 7), 2 False (p. 2), 3 True (p. 9), 4 False (p. 10), 5 False (p. 13), 6 True (p. 16), 7 False (p. 16), 8 True (p. 22).

- Ask the children to draw a picture that Alice could stick in the book she is making. Make sure they are aware of its title, *Horses, Ponies and Dogs*.

Extension activities

- Ask the children to fold a piece of paper into four. They should create on it four wallpaper designs using only two colours for each.

- The children could design a bedroom for themselves and label what they would put in it.

WORKSHEET 2
Personal Response

Activity *Exploring a character's emotions*

- Discuss how Alice feels at key points during the story. Ask the children how they would have felt.

- Talk about the words listed on the worksheet. Make sure the children can read and understand them all.

- Ask the children to choose from the words on the list and decide which feeling is most appropriate to each picture.

Extension activity

- Ask the children to cut out the four pictures, separating the text from the pictures. These could then be used for a sequencing activity.

Cutting and Sticking   Name _____   Date _____

Write **true** or **false** next to these sentences.

1. Dad let Alice help straight away. _____

2. Jess didn't want to help. _____

3. Alice was good at cutting and sticking. _____

4. Alice cut her finger with the scissors. _____

5. It was snowing outside. _____

6. Spike chewed the paper. _____

7. Alice put all the paper in Spike's basket. _____

8. Alice was good at clearing up. _____

Draw a picture that Alice could stick in her book.

How did Alice feel at different points in the story?
Use some of the words in the list to complete the sentences.

lonely   upset   angry   happy   worried   annoyed   jealous   pleased

| When Alice saw Dad and Jess putting up wallpaper, she felt | When Dad told Alice to go downstairs, she felt | When Alice tore the picture into tiny pieces, she felt |

_____ .   _____ .   _____ .

When Alice stuck the picture neatly in her

scrapbook, she felt _____ .

Draw a picture to match the caption.

Parrot Talk

Author June Crebbin

Illustrator Peter Kavanagh

Strand contemporary

Towards Independence: A

Other books in the strand at this stage

- Cutting and Sticking
- Strawberry Picking

Introducing the book

- Talk about the cover, including the title and blurb. Invite predictions about the book's contents.

After reading the book

- Talk about the care of pets and what happens to them if their owners go away for a few days or for a week or more.
- Discuss how the children think they learnt to talk.

WORKSHEET 1
Reading Development

Activity *Comprehension: answering questions*

- Ask the children to read through the questions and then to try answering them orally from memory before completing the worksheet. Some children may need to refer to the text to check their answers.
- Then the children should complete the worksheet. The more skilled children should refer to the text at this stage to check whether they were right.

Extension activity

- Ask each of the children to make up one quiz question about the book. Use these as a new quiz for this or another group.

WORKSHEET 2
Personal Response

Activity *Extension of ideas*

- Draw the children's attention to page 17, where everyone tries to get Sidney to talk.
- Ask the children for their own ideas about what Sidney might say. Make a list of suggestions.
- The worksheet can then be completed using these ideas.

Extension activity

- Discuss what animals might say if they could speak. Examples they could talk about are a dog at the vet's, a lion at the zoo, a goldfish at a fair and a horse in a race. The children could draw one or two animals and write what they might say in speech bubbles.

Parrot Talk   Name _____   Date _____

Answer these questions.
Check your answers in the book.

1. Who said Ben was a copycat? (page 2)

_____

2. Why did Sidney come to stay with the family? (page 5)

_____

3. Why did Mum take Sidney to the vet? (page 13)

_____

4. Where was the book sale held? (page 18)

_____

5. Ben said two things to Emma's teacher (page 22) and two things to his mother (page 24). Write them in the speech bubbles.

Parrot Talk   Name _____   Date _____

> Everyone tried to get Sidney to talk. Dad kept
> saying, "Who's a pretty boy then?"
>   Tom and Emma kept trying all of Sidney's
> favourite sayings.   (page 17)

What would you like Sidney to say?

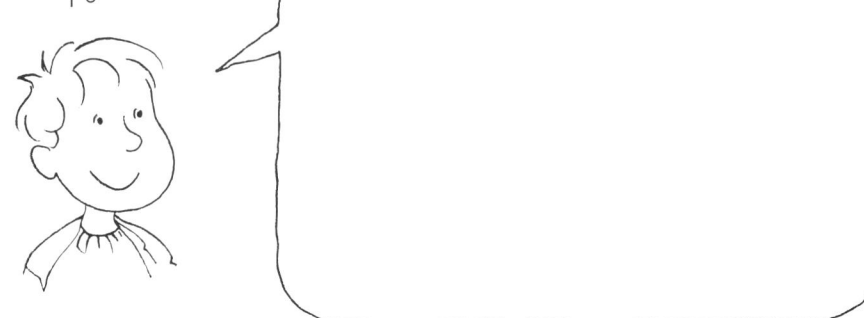

Which of these sayings might Ben copy first?

© CUP 1996. Original artwork by Peter Kavanagh.

Strawberry Picking

Author June Crebbin

Illustrator Peter Kavanagh

Strand contemporary

Other books in the strand at this stage

- Cutting and Sticking
- Parrot Talk

Introducing the book

- Talk about the cover, including the title and blurb. Invite predictions about the book's contents.
- Discuss hay fever. Does anyone suffer from it? What effects does it have?

After reading the book

- If appropriate, ask the children who has been strawberry picking and discuss what happened.
- Ask if anyone has been lost by their family.
- Encourage children who have been lost to say what happened.

WORKSHEET 1
Reading Development

Activity *Matching and ordering sentences*

- Ask the children to match the sentences to the right section of the story. They may be able to do this from the given text and memory or they may need to refer to the text.
- The children will then need to order the strips of text in the correct box. They could work in pairs, using one worksheet for each pair.

Extension activity

- The pair could use the strips of text to help them retell the story to another pair or the teacher, or to record it on tape.

WORKSHEET 2
Personal Response

Activity *Relating text to personal experience*

- Discuss what strategies Tom might have used to look after Ben in the past – refer to page 6: 'He knew what to do.'
- Before they complete the worksheet, the children should imagine they have the task of looking after a younger child at home for a while. Ask them who it might be (e.g. brother, sister, friend).
- Discuss what kinds of things the children might do. Make a list of toys and activities (e.g. singing, looking at a picture book). Help the children to clarify the reasons for their choices.
- If the children can't think of a younger child they could look after, suggest that they complete the worksheet as if they were looking after Ben.

Strawberry Picking   Name _____   Date _____

Cut out the sentences and stick them in order in the right box.

Tom kept an eye on Ben while Dad waited in line.  	Dad kept an eye on Ben while Tom picked strawberries. 

They walked along the side of the field.	Ben looked at the strawberries. He picked one out of a box.
One of Tom's friends came into the shop.	They both went to look for him.
He took a strawberry from every box.	Then they found him, fast asleep under a tree.
They walked up and down the rows of strawberry pickers.	Suddenly, there was a shout.

Strawberry Picking   Name _____   Date _____

Tom had to look after his
baby brother Ben.

How would you look after a
younger child?

Who are you looking after?	Draw two toys that you would use.
Name _____ _____ Age _____	

Draw and write about what you would do together if you had no toys.

Draw here.	I would We would do this because

The Dog Show

Author June Crebbin

Illustrator Peter Kavanagh

Strand contemporary

Other books in the strand at this stage

- The Pyjama Party
- The Special Cake

Introducing the book

- Talk about the cover, including the title and blurb. Invite predictions about the book's contents.

- Discuss what a dog show is. Ask if the children have ever been to one.

After reading the book

- What do the children think makes a good dog? You could list the children's responses under Appearance, Behaviour and Feelings (i.e. how they relate to and feel about the pet).

- Invite the children to tell stories about their dogs or other pets.

WORKSHEET 1
Reading Development

Activity *Comprehension: answering questions*

- The worksheet focuses on two different sections of the story, pages 3–6 and 21–27. The children could look at these in pairs, using the page numbers given.

- They should discuss the answers to the questions, checking them in the book before writing their answers down.

Extension activities

- Ask the children to design a winning rosette. Draw their attention to page 31, where Spike receives a red rosette.

- The children could imagine that they are judges at a dog show. They could write a list of questions that they might ask an owner about their dog.

WORKSHEET 2
Personal Response

Activity *Ranking sentences*

- Make sure the children understand the practice of giving a rosette as a mark of distinction.

- Ask the children to discuss which were the funniest bits in the story, giving reasons for their choices, before doing the worksheet.

Extension activity

- Cut out and make a display or booklet of the children's drawings of 'the funniest bit'. Ask other children who have not done the worksheet to identify the points in the story illustrated in the drawings.

The Dog Show

Name _____ Date _____

Getting ready

What did Alice do to get Spike looking nice?

(pages 3–5)

What did Spike do?

(page 6)

At the dog show

What did Spike do perfectly?

(page 21)

What special trick did Spike do?

(page 27)

Which of these bits of the story
do you think was the funniest?

Draw a red rosette by your first choice,
a blue rosette by your second choice, and
a yellow rosette by your third choice.

Spike shook himself.

Black hair whizzed all over the bathroom. It stuck to the walls. It stuck to the towels. It stuck to the floor.
(page 6)

Spike saw the cat too. He leapt in the air to get it. The cat leapt in the air too, out of the boy's arms, and ran straight across the field. (page 16)

Alice stared at the feather on the vet's hat. She didn't know what to say. Then, suddenly, the wind lifted not only the feather but the whole hat, and sent it flying across the field. (page 25)

Draw the funniest bit here.

The Pyjama Party

Author June Crebbin

Illustrator Peter Kavanagh

Strand contemporary

Towards Independence: B

Other books in the strand at this stage

- The Dog Show
- The Special Cake

Introducing the book

- Talk about the cover, including the title and blurb. Invite predictions about the book's contents.
- Discuss sending invitations. Ask the children what information is needed on all of them.

After reading the book

- Brainstorm the kinds of parties the children might go to throughout the year (e.g. birthday, New Year, Christmas).
- Discuss the variety of birthday parties that the children have been to.

WORKSHEET 1
Reading Development

Activity *Bookmaking and illustration*

- The children will need a photocopy of the book-making activity on page 31.
- The ghost story told by Dad is re-created on the worksheet. The children should follow the instructions to make their book. Then they should illustrate it. This could then be taken home and read.
- Talk about blurbs before the children attempt to write one for the ghost story.

Extension activity

- Get the children to make other books based on stories they know well.

WORKSHEET 2
Personal Response

Activity *Exploring a character's emotions*

- For the first half of the worksheet, discuss why Tom didn't want to join in Emma's party.
- Make sure the children appreciate that there could be several reasons.
- For the second half, ask the children whether there have been times when they didn't want to join in something. Ask them to tell their story to a partner before completing the worksheet.

Extension activity

- The children could write down all the 'feeling' words about parties that they can think of, sorting them into two columns: 'Good' and 'Nasty'.

2

Every night a ghost flew round and round the house.

3

Every night the ghost tapped on the window, trying to get in.

4

The ghost flew round and round the house so much that it got dizzy.

1

Once upon a time, there was a house on a hill.

A haunted house.

A Ghost Story

Illustrated by

5

So it stopped flying round the house, and it flew far away, as far as the moon, …

6

…and was never seen again.

This book is about

ISBN 0-521-24871-X

Price:

© Cambridge University Press 1996

The Pyjama Party

Name _____ Date _____

Tick the reasons which you think are right.
Then write two reasons of your own.

Tom didn't want to join in Emma's party because...

☐ he felt shy.

☐ he felt jealous.

☐ he felt silly in pyjamas.

☐ he didn't like Emma's friends.

he _____ .

he _____ .

Have you ever wanted **not** to join in something?
Draw and write about it.

Draw here.	Write here.

© CUP 1996. Original artwork by Peter Kavanagh.

Worksheet 2 Personal Response   91

The Special Cake

Author June Crebbin

Illustrator Peter Kavanagh

Strand contemporary

Towards Independence: B

Other books in the strand at this stage

- The Dog Show
- The Pyjama Party

Introducing the book

- Talk about the cover, including the title and blurb. Invite predictions about the book's contents.
- Look at the language of recipe books with the children.
- Point out that recipes usually start with the ingredients, often in the order of use, and then give the method.
- Make sure that the children know and understand words such as 'ingredients', 'utensils' and 'method'.

After reading the book

- Discuss bird-tables, bird-watching and bird-feeding. What can the children tell you about the way different birds feed?

WORKSHEET 1
Reading Development

Activity *Sequencing and cloze*

- Before the children begin the cloze, talk about the key verbs in the first three strips (i.e. 'pour', 'tip', 'put', 'stir'). Ask the children to circle the key verbs in the last three strips (i.e. 'leave', 'store', 'add', 'stir').
- The children should then complete the cloze, referring to the book if necessary.

Answers   fat, cake, cheese, mixture, tin, kitchen.

- Finally, they should cut out the instructions and try to put them in order without looking at the book. Then let them use the book to check.

Extension activity

- The children could make a list of the ingredients for the bird-cake. This could be illustrated and taken home.

WORKSHEET 2
Personal Response

Activity *Inventing a cake*

- Talk to the children about the special ingredients needed for the bird-cake.
- Ask the children which animal they would like to make a special cake for – for example, a dog or a horse. What special ingredients would they need?
- Remind the children of *Sophie's Box* by John Prater (Becoming a Reader: B) in which a scare-crow makes a cake for a goat. Stress that the recipe is a fantasy one which in real life would probably be unsafe for the animal.
- Discuss how they would make their cake.
- Emphasise the need to choose ingredients that are known to be liked by their animal and that are safe. Explain that the children must not use their recipe at home without first asking for advice.

The Special Cake

Name _____   Date _____

Jess made a bird-cake. Use words in the list to fill in the gaps in the recipe, then cut the instructions out and put them in the right order.

tin	fat	cheese
kitchen	mixture	cake

Pour hot _____ over the mixture so that the ingredients stick together.

Tip the bowl upside down and the _____ should drop onto the plate.

Put the nuts, dried fruit and grated _____ into a bowl. Stir the ingredients.

Leave the _____ until it is cold.

Store it in a _____ .

Next add any _____ scraps and stir everything together again.

The Special Cake   Name _____   Date _____

Who would you like to make a special cake for?

Write the ingredients in the bowl.

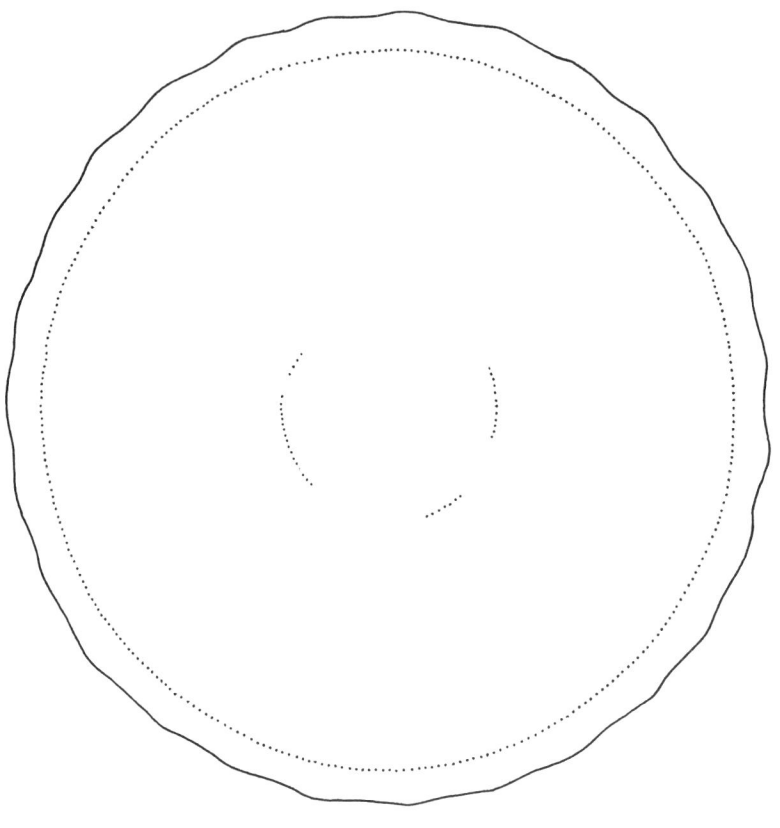

Draw the animal here.

Write a recipe for your cake.

1. Mix together	2. Add
3. Then	4. Finally

A Cat for Keeps

Author June Crebbin

Illustrator Peter Kavanagh

Strand contemporary

Towards Independence: C

Other books in the strand at this stage

- Don't Be Late!
- Spike and the Concert

Introducing the book

- Talk about the cover, including the title and blurb. Invite predictions about the book's contents.

After reading the book

- Discuss why Tom wanted a pet and his feelings about the kitten.
- Discuss trips to the theatre, cinema and so on. Encourage the children to describe what they saw and what they felt like.

WORKSHEET 1
Reading Development

Activity *Classification*

- Explain that the children should consider a number of things that Tom saw and then put them into three different lists, referring to the text as necessary.
- The children can add to the lists if they want to.
- For the word-web the children need to identify the words in the text that describe the kitten (see pages 20, 21, 26, 29 and 32).

   Answers black, lucky, stray, sweet, thin, tiny, weak.

Extension activity

- Ask the children to divide a piece of paper into four by folding or ruling lines. Then they should think of four places – for example, forest, bedroom, bus station, playground – and brainstorm the different things they would expect to see in each place. This could be done individually, and then the lists could be compared.

WORKSHEET 2
Personal Response

Activity *Completing an attributes chart*

- Draw the children's attention to the role of the three cats in the story: Grandma's fat tabby, Tommy the Cat and Lucky.
- Ask the children to think of things that the three cats have in common (e.g. they all have fur), and then of things about them that are different (e.g. they are not all black).

Extension activity

- The children could draw up a similar data sheet to consider the characteristics of the people in the book.

A Cat for Keeps

Name _____   Date _____

What things did Tom see on his trip?
Write these things in the right list.

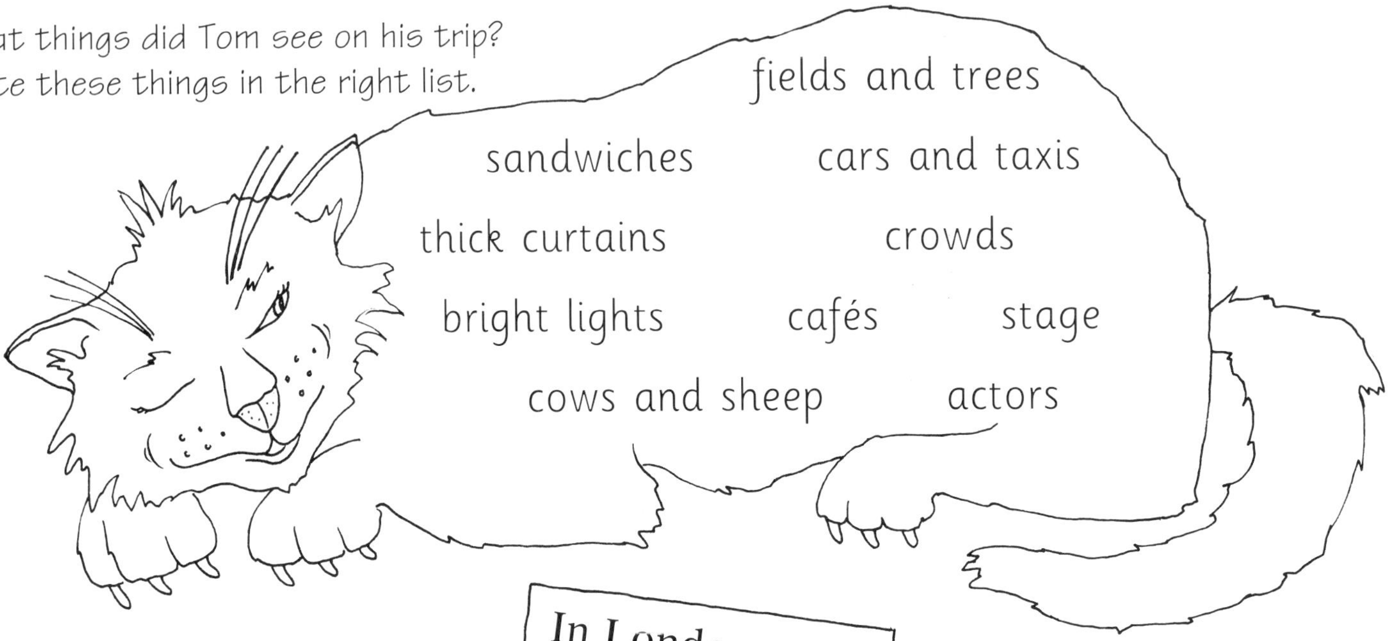

fields and trees

sandwiches   cars and taxis

thick curtains   crowds

bright lights   cafés   stage

cows and sheep   actors

In London

On the train

At the theatre

What was Uncle Jack's kitten like?
Look at pages 20, 21, 26, 29 and 32.
Put the key words on the word-web.

kitten

Worksheet 1 Reading Development

A Cat for Keeps

Name _____ Date _____

There are three cats in the story.

Grandma's fat tabby

Tommy the Cat

Lucky the kitten

Fill in this chart about the cats using ✓ and ✗.
Some of the answers are easy. Some you will have to think about!

	Grandma's cat	Tommy the Cat	Lucky *before* Uncle Jack found her	Lucky *after* Uncle Jack found her
It is a real cat.				
It is a happy cat.				
It purrs.				
It dances and climbs.				
Everyone loves it.				
It is warm and soft.				
It is weak and thin.				

Don't Be Late!

Author June Crebbin

Illustrator Peter Kavanagh

Strand contemporary

Other books in the strand at this stage

- A Cat for Keeps
- Spike and the Concert

Introducing the book

- Talk about the cover, including the title and blurb. Invite predictions about the book's contents.

After reading the book

- Ask the children if they or their family have been late for an important occasion. What is their story?
- Brainstorm the sort of things that happen at weddings and how different cultures celebrate them.

WORKSHEET 1
Reading Development

Activity *Sequencing events to make a game*

- If possible, show the children a board game that has brief instructions so that you can model the activity.
- Ask the children to look at the large box numbered 3 on the worksheet. They should use the instructions already in the box and the picture clue numbered 3 to recall what happened at that point on the journey.
- Do the same for the other four large numbered boxes.
- Ask the children to complete the boxes in their own words.
- To play the game, the children will need a counter each and a dice.

Extension activity

- Encourage the children to create another game, based on a journey, on the back of the sheet. This could be from home to school or from home to the seaside, or a fantasy game based on a story such as *The Shopping Basket* by John Burningham (Jonathan Cape/Red Fox) or *On the Way Home* by Jill Murphy (Walker Books).

WORKSHEET 2
Personal Response

Activity *Relating text to personal experience*

- Ask the children to look through the book and find references to the fact that it was important to Emma to be a bridesmaid at the wedding. Discuss why it was important for her.
- Talk with the children about occasions when they have worried about being late.
- Before the children begin the worksheet, ask them to talk through each box as if they were Emma.
- If any child has never experienced being late, they could invent a scenario or retell the story from Emma's point of view.

Don't Be Late! Name _____ Date _____

In each numbered box, write what happened. Use the pictures to help you.
Then play the game.

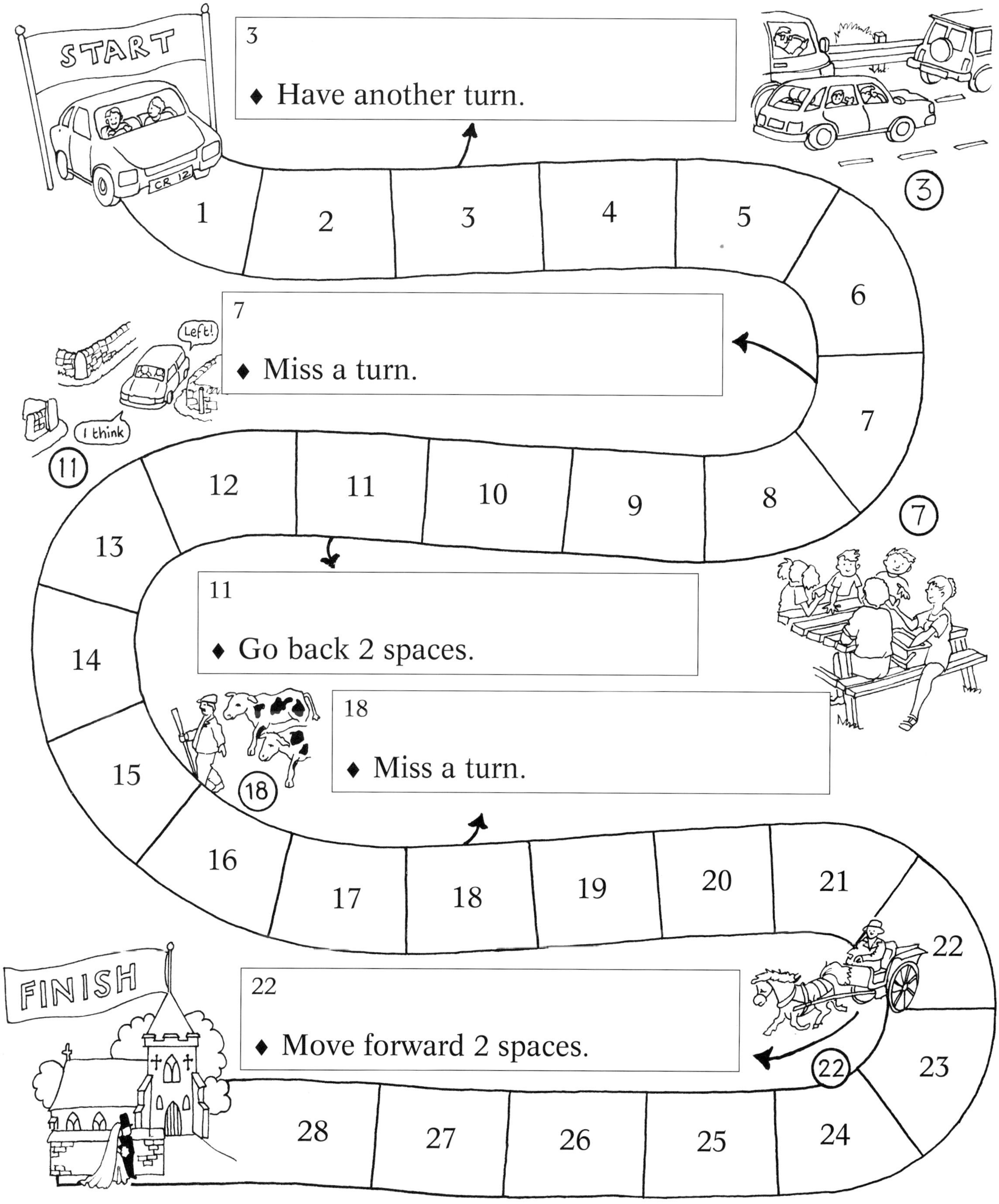

START

3
♦ Have another turn.

1 2 3 4 5 6 7

③

7
♦ Miss a turn.

Left!
I think
⑪

12 11 10 9 8

⑦

11
♦ Go back 2 spaces.

13 14 15 16

18
♦ Miss a turn.

⑱

17 18 19 20 21

22

22
♦ Move forward 2 spaces.

⑳

FINISH

28 27 26 25 24 23

Don't Be Late!

Name _____ Date _____

Have you ever thought that you were going to be
late for something important?
Draw or write a story map to show what happened.
Then write your story on another piece of paper.

START

Where were you going?

Why was it important to you?

Then what happened?

What happened to make you late?

How did it end? Did you arrive on time?

© CUP 1996. Original artwork by Peter Kavanagh.

Spike and the Concert

Author June Crebbin

Illustrator Peter Kavanagh

Strand contemporary

Towards Independence: C

Other books in the strand at this stage

- A Cat for Keeps
- Don't Be Late!

Introducing the book

- Talk about the cover, including the title and blurb. Invite predictions about the book's contents.
- Discuss what a concert is.

After reading the book

- Build upon any experiences the children may have had of going to or being part of a concert performance.
- Look at pictures of musical instruments and see if the children can name them.

WORKSHEET 1
Reading Development

Activity *Finding information; writing captions*

- Ask the children to write under the picture of each character what that person did. They should try to do this first without referring to the text. Then they can use the page numbers to check their answers in the book.
- Then ask them who made the most noise.

Extension activity

- Ask the children to draw a picture of Spike in the middle of a piece of paper and then to write around the picture all the words and phrases they can think of that describe Spike.

WORKSHEET 2
Personal Response

Activity *Exploring a character's actions*

- Ask the children to decide whose viewpoint the story is mainly told from. How do they know?
- Draw the children's attention to the role of Spike in the story.
- Discuss the various situations he finds himself in. Ask the children why they think he acted as he did.
- After discussion about Spike's feelings, ask the children to take on the role of Spike and complete the thought bubbles.

Extension activity

- Ask the children to retell the story from Dad's viewpoint or from Emma's.

Spike and the Concert

Name _____ Date _____

What did everyone do at the concert?

choir (page 22) 	Mrs Fraser (page 23) 

Jess (page 23) 	two girls (page 22) 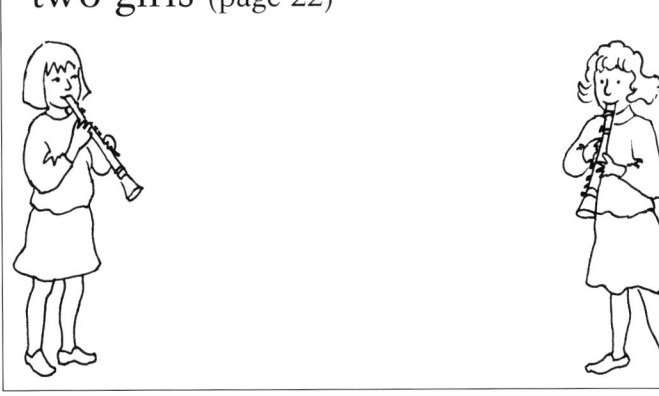

Emma (page 6) 	audience (page 26) 

Spike (page 24)

 *Who do you think made the most noise?*

Spike and the Concert

CAMBRIDGE READING

What is Spike thinking?
Complete the thought bubbles.

I like getting out of the garden because

I hate it when they won't let me come upstairs because

I was so pleased to see Jess near the Town Hall, but

When Jess started to play I joined in because

The Big Shrink

Author Rosemary Hayes

Illustrator Ian Newsham

Strand fantasy

Other Mr Mulch books

- Mr Mulch's Magic Mixtures
- The Amazing Mr Mulch
- The Magic Sword

Towards Independence: A

Other books in the strand at this stage

- The Grabbing Bird
- The Treasure Cave

Introducing the book

- Talk about the cover, including the title and blurb. Invite predictions about the book's contents.
- Discuss the word 'shrink' and devise a definition together.

After reading the book

- Ask the children to say what problems they would be likely to have in the classroom if they shrank to a few centimetres high.
- Make a word-web for words that mean roughly the same as 'big' and another for 'small'.

WORKSHEET 1
Reading Development

Activity *Sequencing events to create a game*

- The children should cut out the instructions and put them in the right place, using the picture cues as a guide. Then they can play the game. Each pair will need counters and a dice.

Answers

| above space 21 | beside space 7 | above space 14 |
| above space 26 | above space 4 | beside space 23 |

Extension activities

- Tell the children to imagine they have shrunk while sitting at their desks and need to get to your table. Ask them to draw their route across the classroom, showing how they used different things to help them.
- The children could each make two lists, one for the biggest creatures they can think of and one for the smallest. Then ask the group to compare their lists.

WORKSHEET 2
Personal Response

Activity *Ranking events: pictures and sentences*

- Ask the children to discuss which parts of the story they thought were the most dangerous for Sam and Jason, explaining their choice.
- Working in pairs, the children should talk about the pictures and the text extracts. Then they should cut out them out and decide which of the four events is the most dangerous. After that they put the rest in order of danger. Make it clear that there are several possible orders.

Extension activity

- Encourage the children to invent a new dangerous moment for Sam and Jason. They should draw the situation and write suitable text for it.

The Big Shrink   Name _____   Date _____

Stick the instructions in the right places. Then play the game.
You need counters and a dice.

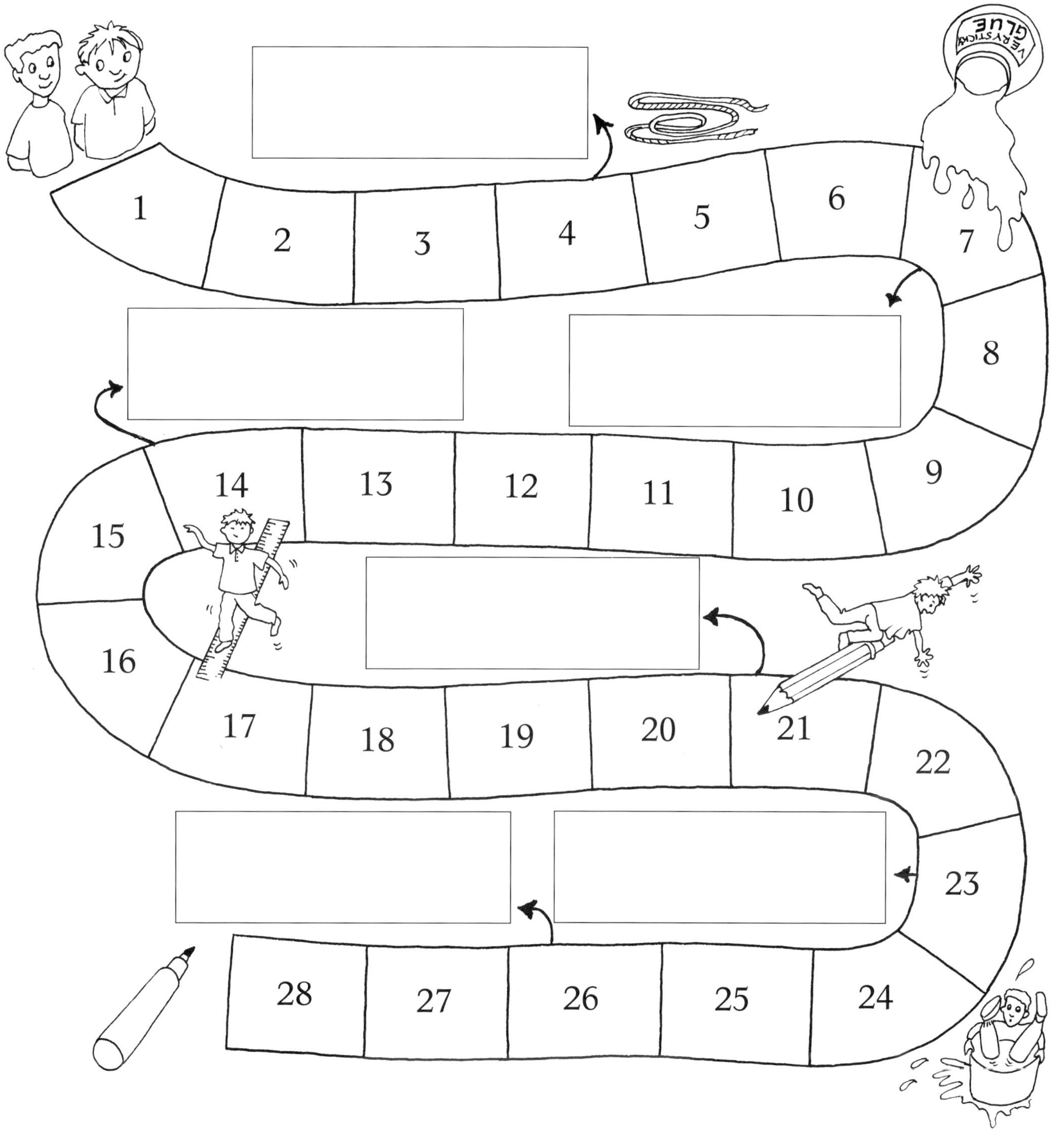

VERY STICKY GLUE

| 1 | 2 | 3 | 4 | 5 | 6 | 7 | 8 | 9 |

| 14 | 13 | 12 | 11 | 10 |

| 15 | | | | | | |

| 16 | 17 | 18 | 19 | 20 | 21 | 22 |

| | 23 |

| 28 | 27 | 26 | 25 | 24 |

You trip over a pencil.	You get stuck in glue.	You use a ruler as a bridge.
◆ Go back 2 spaces.	◆ Miss a turn.	◆ Go forward 3 spaces.
You creep across the teacher's table.	You climb up a piece of string.	You fall into a pot of paint.
◆ Go forward 2 spaces.	◆ Have another turn.	◆ Miss a turn.

The Big Shrink   Name _____   Date _____

Which moments in the story do you think were the most dangerous for Sam and Jason?

Cut out the pictures and sentences below and put them in order, starting with the most dangerous situation.

Jason jumped up as high as he could and caught the string. Very carefully, he started to climb.

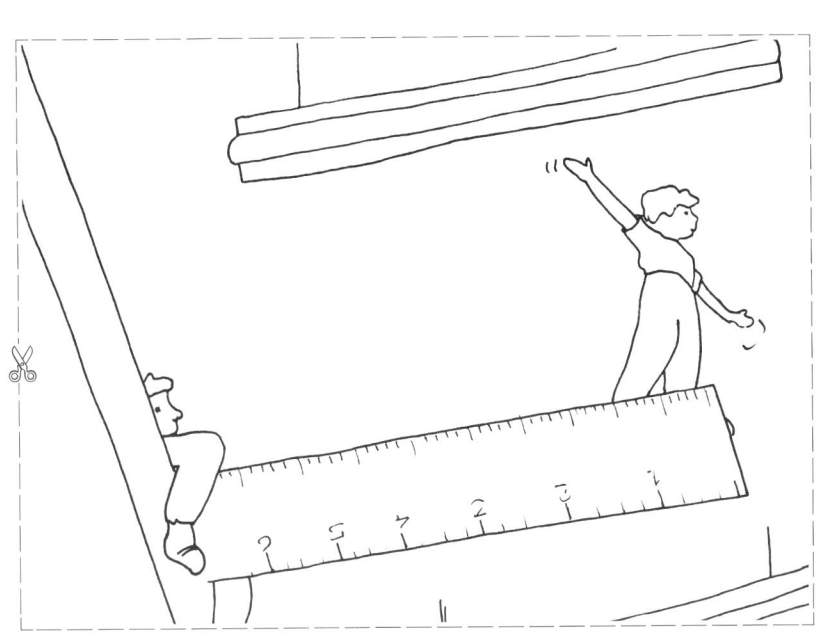

"Help!" shrieked Jason and Sam. They stood flat against a wall as all the giant children crashed past them to the door.

The Grabbing Bird

Author Rosemary Hayes

Illustrator Ian Newsham

Strand fantasy

Towards Independence: A

Other books in the strand at this stage
- The Big Shrink
- The Treasure Cave

Introducing the book

- Talk about the cover, including the title and blurb. Invite predictions about the book's contents.

After reading the book

- Discuss the grabbing bird's motives. Why does it want the stone? Brainstorm ideas with the class and list the better ones. Then ask individual children to say which idea they like best.

- Ask the children how they know that the story is a fantasy.

WORKSHEET 1
Reading Development

Activity *Comprehension: crossword*

- Talk to the children about crosswords, showing them an example. Make sure they understand the difference between 'Across' and 'Down' clues.

- Remind the children that when they fill in a crossword, they should always write one letter in each box.

- Point out that the first letter of each word is given as a clue. When they have decided on the correct word, they should trace over the first letter and then continue the word.

- Show them how to answer the first clue, referring to the book for the answer and for the correct spelling.

Answers *Across:* 1 grabbing bird, 4 planets, 6 stone, 8 castle. *Down:* 2 bouncing, 3 guards, 5 Sophie, 7 tree.

WORKSHEET 2
Personal Response

Activity *Exploring a character's emotions*

- Ask the children to look back at the story and look for evidence that the people on the planet wanted to stop bouncing. Why might the planet people have felt this way? Would the people have felt the same if they were able to bounce, but did not have to do so all the time?

- Discuss why Sophie might enjoy bouncing. What might she say about it in her speech bubble? The children should fill in all the speech bubbles to show why they think some characters in the story enjoyed bouncing while others didn't. The children could then compare what they have written.

Extension activity

- In pairs or small groups, the children should imagine that they can bounce. In what ways would their lives be more difficult or more fun if they had to bounce? What would they enjoy doing if they could *choose* to bounce when they wanted to?

The Grabbing Bird   Name _____   Date _____

Use the book to help you do this crossword.

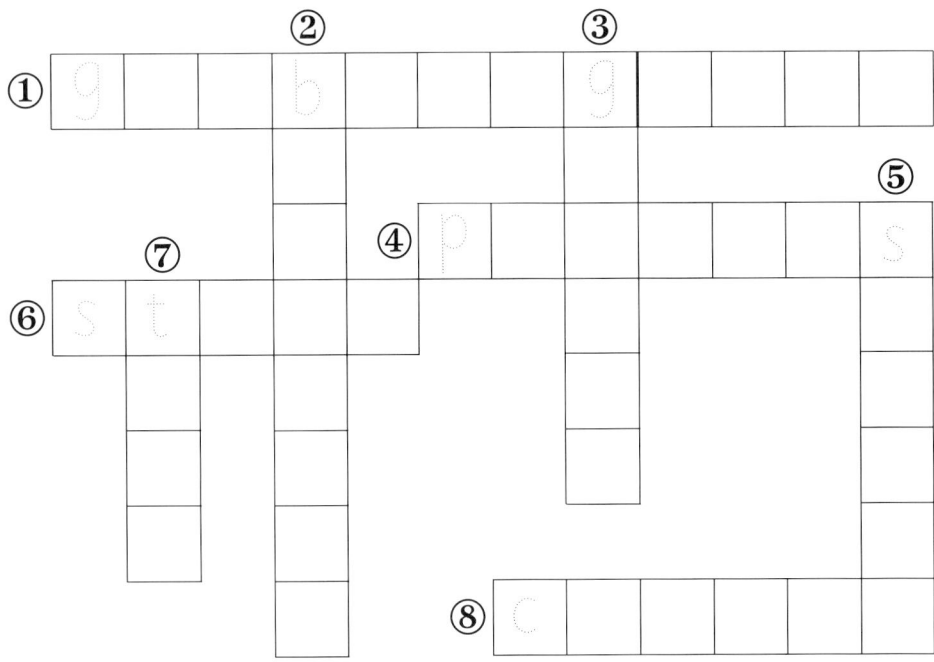

Across

1. The creature who stole the stone. (two words) (page 19)
4. Tom and Sophie bounced off these in space. (page 8)
6. The grabbing bird dropped this. (page 4)
8. The bouncy building on the hill. (page 13)

Down

2. The people on the planet were doing this. (page 10)
3. They were fat and sleepy. (page 14)
5. Tom's sister. (page 2)
7. The grabbing bird hit this. (page 21)

108   Worksheet 1 Reading Development   © CUP 1996. Original artwork by Ian Newsham.

The Grabbing Bird   Name _____   Date _____

Finish the sentences in the speech bubbles.

I like bouncing because

I don't like bouncing because

I like bouncing because

I don't like bouncing because

The Treasure Cave

Author Rosemary Hayes

Illustrator Ian Newsham

Strand fantasy

Towards Independence: A

Other books in the strand at this stage

- The Big Shrink
- The Grabbing Bird

Introducing the book

- Talk about the cover, including the title and blurb. Invite predictions about the book's contents.

- Discuss what a magician might be. What do the children think one would look like? What might a magician do?

After reading the book

- Ask the children which event they thought was the most exciting.

WORKSHEET 1
Reading Development

Activity *Classification: descriptions*

- Point out that the circles on the worksheet include the names of colours as well as of characters.

- The children should colour the characters the appropriate colour first.

- Read the descriptions with the children. Explain that they may need to re-read the story to find out which character or characters each description fits best.

- Then they should colour the descriptions as appropriate.

Answers *Blue:* happy; scared; terrified. *Red:* grumpy; wore a long cloak; not very clever; his voice echoed . . .; lots of hairy legs. *Yellow:* dancing, jumping and shouting; walked stiffly towards her; shadows of people.

Extension activity

- The children could draw their own picture of the magician and then write in a large speech bubble the spell they think he cast on the guards long ago.

WORKSHEET 2
Personal Response

Activity *Choosing an exciting plot point*

- Talk to the children about taking photographs. How do people choose which pictures to take?

- Ask the children to pretend that they are hiding in the cave with a camera during Sarah and Marnie's adventure. Explain that they can take only one photograph. They have to decide which part of the story they would most like to record with a snapshot.

- The children could compare their picture and caption with those drawn by the rest of the group, and then explain to one another why they made their choice.

Extension activity

- What other pictures of Sarah and Marnie's adventure would the children choose to take?

The Treasure Cave

Name _____ Date _____

Who are these words describing:
the magician, Sarah or the guards?

Colour each character.
Then colour each box of words the right colour for the character.

grumpy

wore a
long cloak

Magician

red

happy

Sarah

blue

dancing,
jumping and
shouting

scared

terrified

not very clever

his voice echoed round
the cave like the roar
of a lion

walked stiffly towards her

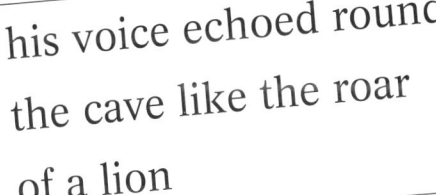
guards

yellow

lots of hairy legs

like the shadows of people

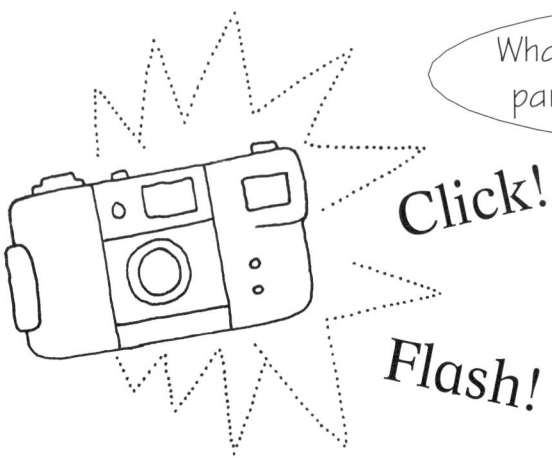

What do you think was the most exciting part of Sarah and Marnie's adventure?

Click!

Flash!

Imagine you are hiding in the cave with a camera and can take one photograph.
Draw the picture that you choose to take and write a caption for it.

Jumble Power

Author Rosemary Hayes

Illustrator Ian Newsham

Strand fantasy

Towards Independence: B

Other books in the strand at this stage
- The Magic Sword
- The Peace Ring

Introducing the book

- Talk about the cover, including the title and blurb. Invite predictions about the book's contents.

After reading the book

- Ask the children what they think about the eating competition. Would it be a good idea to hold one? Why?

- Discuss ideas for futuristic gadgets that could be used in the kitchen to provide instant food.

- Ask the children about the varieties of food they have eaten (e.g. Chinese, Indian, McDonalds). Which kind do they enjoy most?

WORKSHEET 1
Reading Development

Activity *Labelling; word grid; syllables*

- Make sure the children can read the food labels on the worksheet.

- Ask the children to match the words to the pictures. They could do this in pairs.

- Explain that in a word grid labels are given as the clues. The children have to count the letters in the labels to find the right place for each word. Suggest that they should start by filling in the words with most letters.

- The more able spellers could be encouraged to write the words under the pictures from memory, using the Look–Cover–Write–Check strategy.

- Tell the children to look at the leopard's question. Answering it will help them to consolidate their understanding of syllables within words.

Answer

```
             t
             r
       p i z z a
             f           c           b
c h o c o l a t e m o u s s e
h           e           r           f
i                       r           b
p                       y           u
s                                   r
                                    g
             s a u s a g e s
                                    r
```

Extension activity

- The children could make up their own word grid, perhaps including their favourite foods.

WORKSHEET 2
Personal Response

Activity *Inventing a machine; labelling*

- Ask the children to look back at the descriptions of the food machines. Which machines would they enjoy using?

- In small groups, they should invent some different types of food machine (e.g. ones serving sweet food, party food, crunchy food, sticky food, Italian food, school dinners). Ask them to discuss what kinds of food would come out of these machines and how the machines would be operated.

- The children should then draw on the worksheet a design for one of the food machines they invented. This might include operating instructions like 'Press', 'Push' and 'Pull' on buttons or levers, and labels for different types of food.

- Then the children should write a list of the kinds of food that would come out of their machine.

Jumble Power Name _____ Date _____

Draw lines from the words to the right pictures.

beefburger

sausages

pizza

chips

chocolate mousse

trifle

curry

Use the words to fill in the word grid.

How many syllables
does each word have?

Jumble Power

Name _____ Date _____

Invent your own food machine and draw it here.
Add labels to show people what each bit does.
Make a list of foods that could come out of it.

Draw here.

Write your list here.

The Magic Sword

Author Rosemary Hayes

Illustrator Ian Newsham

Strand fantasy

Other Mr Mulch books

- Mr Mulch's Magic Mixtures
- The Amazing Mr Mulch
- The Big Shrink

Towards Independence: B

Other books in the strand at this stage

- Jumble Power
- The Peace Ring

Introducing the book

- Talk about the cover, including the title and blurb. Invite predictions about the book's contents.

- Ask the children to recall any other stories about Mr Mulch that they have read.

After reading the book

- Ask the children about the sword's magic powers. What did it make happen that was out of the ordinary?

- Brainstorm the emotions of the children in Mr Mulch's group at the most dramatic points in the story.

- What do the children think happened to the ghosts and to the sword at the end of the story?

WORKSHEET 1
Reading Development

Activity *Cloze: vocabulary extension*

- The words and the cloze passage are taken verbatim from pages 27 and 28. Ask the children to look at the pictures on these two pages. Help them recall this part of the story.

- The cloze concentrates on movement words. The children should try to define each word by describing each movement. Point out that all but one of the verbs end with the pattern -ed.

- Some children could cover the list of words at the top of the worksheet and try to write the words independently. Others may need to write the words on slips of paper first and move them around on the cloze to find the right places for them. They can then copy the answers in.

- Tell the children to refer to pages 27 and 28 to check their answers.

WORKSHEET 2
Personal Response

Activity *Exploring characters' reactions*

- Read the speech bubble at the top of the worksheet with the children and ask them who said these words. Discuss why Karen's mum made the comment and ask whether they agree with her.

- Divide the children into groups of four. In the groups, each child takes on the role of one of Samantha, Andrew, Salim and Karen. After looking at the text for help, each child should tell the others what event they remember best about the trip to the castle. The child playing Samantha might choose riding the horse, for example. Encourage them to discuss whether the four characters would remember the same things.

- It may be appropriate for some children to do this activity in pairs instead of in groups.

- The children should then write in the speech bubbles particular memories of the trip for each character. They may do this either in their original role or as a group.

Talk about what these words mean.

tumbled

picked

reared

dropped

swooped

dangled

stared

hurtling

Use the words to fill in the spaces.

Suddenly, there was a great WOOSHING sound.

The horse _____ up in fright and Samantha _____ off its back. The other children _____ as Mr Mulch came _____ through the air. He _____ down on Sir Thomas and _____ him up on the point of the sword.

Sir Thomas was so surprised that he _____ Andrew and Christopher.

Then Mr Mulch _____ Sir Thomas over the hole and shook the sword.

I bet you didn't have much fun.
Not with that supply teacher.
He looks really dull.

Do you think that these children in Mr Mulch's group would agree?
What do you think they might remember best about the trip?

I remember

Samantha

What I liked best was when

Andrew

That makes me think of

Salim

I enjoyed

Karen

The Peace Ring

Author Rosemary Hayes

Illustrator Ian Newsham

Strand fantasy

Towards Independence: B

Other books in the strand at this stage
- Jumble Power
- The Magic Sword

Introducing the book

- Talk about the cover, including the title and blurb. Invite predictions about the book's contents.

After reading the book

- Have the children ever made friends again with anyone after they have disagreed or had a fight?

- Ask the children what they know about disagreements. Can they suggest good ways of making up?

WORKSHEET 1
Reading Development

Activity *Cloze: vocabulary extension*

- Make sure the children understand that Tallic's speech gives the context for all the events in the book.

- Check that the children can read all the words in the list before they start the cloze.

- Read Tallic's speech aloud, pausing at the first two gaps to allow them to guess what the missing words are.

- Some children could cover the list of words at the top of the worksheet and try to write the words independently.

- Others may need to write the words on slips of paper first and move them around on the cloze to find the right places for them. They can then copy the answers in.

- Tell the children to refer to pages 13 and 14 to check their answers.

WORKSHEET 2
Personal Response

Activity *Explanatory writing*

- Divide the children into small groups (six in each is ideal). Explain that half of each group should pretend to be root-dwellers and the other half tree-dwellers. Each half should talk together about the advantages of their particular lifestyle. Then rearrange the children into pairs, putting one root-dweller with one tree-dweller. The two in turn explain the advantages of their lifestyle to the other.

- The children should complete the speech bubbles, using some of the ideas they have shared.

Extension activity

- The disadvantages of being a root-dweller or a tree-dweller could be explored in the same way.

The Peace Ring

Name _____ Date _____

Fill in the missing words using the list below.

roots	believe	trees
leader	happy	Peace
brother	fighting	stolen
sky	returned	

My name is Tallic and I am the _____ of the people who live down here in the _____ . We are called the root-dwellers.

Up above, in the branches of the _____ , live the tree-dwellers. They are led by my _____ , Frond – you can see him on the screen. When we had the _____ Ring, we lived in peace. Its light makes everyone _____ , you see.

But one day, the Peace Ring disappeared. Frond said we'd _____ it. Of course we hadn't, but the tree-dwellers didn't _____ us. Ever since then we have been _____ . Frond has said that we will never see the _____ again until the Peace Ring is _____ .

When you have finished, check your answers in the book.

Worksheet 1 Reading Development

The Peace Ring

Name _____ Date _____

Think of some good reasons for living as a tree-dweller
or as a root-dweller.
Write some of your ideas in the speech bubbles.

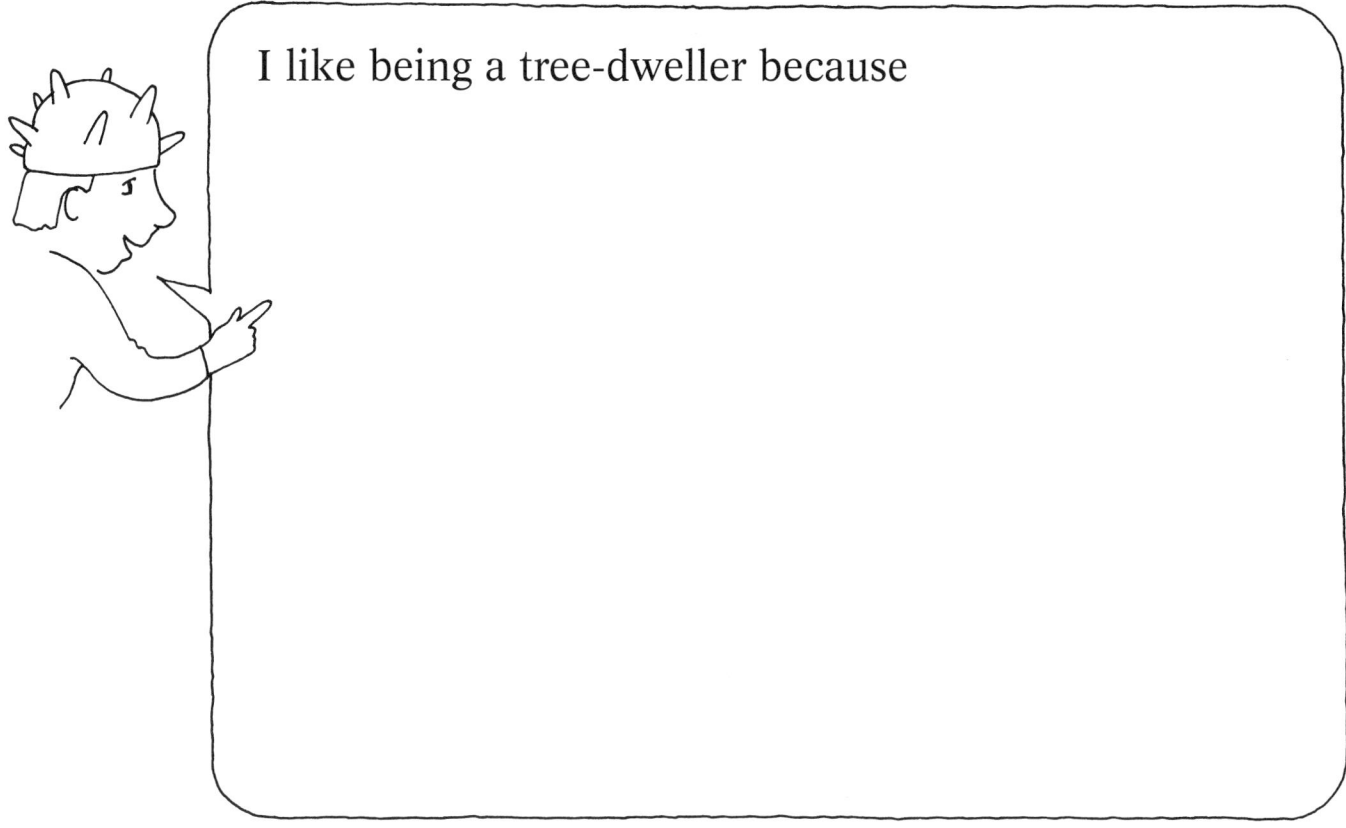

I like being a tree-dweller because

I enjoy being a root-dweller because

Mr Mulch's Magic Mixtures

Author Rosemary Hayes

Illustrator Ian Newsham

Strand fantasy

Other Mr Mulch books

- The Amazing Mr Mulch
- The Big Shrink
- The Magic Sword

Towards Independence: C

Other books in the strand at this stage

- The Amazing Mr Mulch
- The Slippery Planet

Introducing the book

- Talk about the cover, including the title and blurb. Invite predictions about the book's contents.
- Ask the children to recall any other stories about Mr Mulch that they have read.

After reading the book

- Ask the children to say what problems and dangers they would meet if they suddenly found that the plants and insects in their garden had grown ten times bigger.
- The children could discuss other stories they know which have a growing or shrinking theme.

WORKSHEET 1
Reading Development

Activity *Making a riddle game; matching text and pictures*

- The children should draw the appropriate creature in each box. They may need to refer to the book for help. Then they cut out the boxes with descriptions in them and match them to the drawings. Finally they stick the descriptions in place on the shaded part above each drawing, using a glue stick. They now have a guessing game that they can take home and read.

Extension activities

- The children could create their own books by using a similar arrangement of drawings and flaps. For this they could draw different animals from those in the book, or choose another theme.
- Ask the children to look at minibeasts through a magnifier so they can see mouthparts and other details.

WORKSHEET 2
Personal Response

Activity *Inventing a magic mixture; labelling*

- Lead a discussion in the group about different sorts of magic mixtures that could be invented (e.g. mixtures that change the colour, shape, sound, scent or texture of objects).
- Using ideas from the discussion if they wish, the children should imagine a magic mixture of their own. Ask them to design an eye-catching label for it. The label should include slogans about the mixture's effect and instructions for its use. Show some bottles with labels as models of design and language.

Mr Mulch's Magic Mixtures Name _____

Draw a picture of each kind of creature.
Cut out the descriptions and stick the shaded edge
on the right picture.

snail	ants	pond-skater
mole	caterpillars	thrush

Jody saw an army of enormous red . . .	A huge monster. It had two waving horns and a slithery, slimy body.	They seemed a mile long and they were as fat as pigs.
The ground beneath them began to shake and a huge snout appeared.	An elegant . . . skimmed across the water towards them.	Something huge and feathery had landed on the potato.

Ask your friends to guess what
each creature is. Then lift the flaps
to show them if they are right.

Mr Mulch's Magic Mixtures   Name _____

Draw and write the label for your own magic mixture.
What does it do? How would you use it?

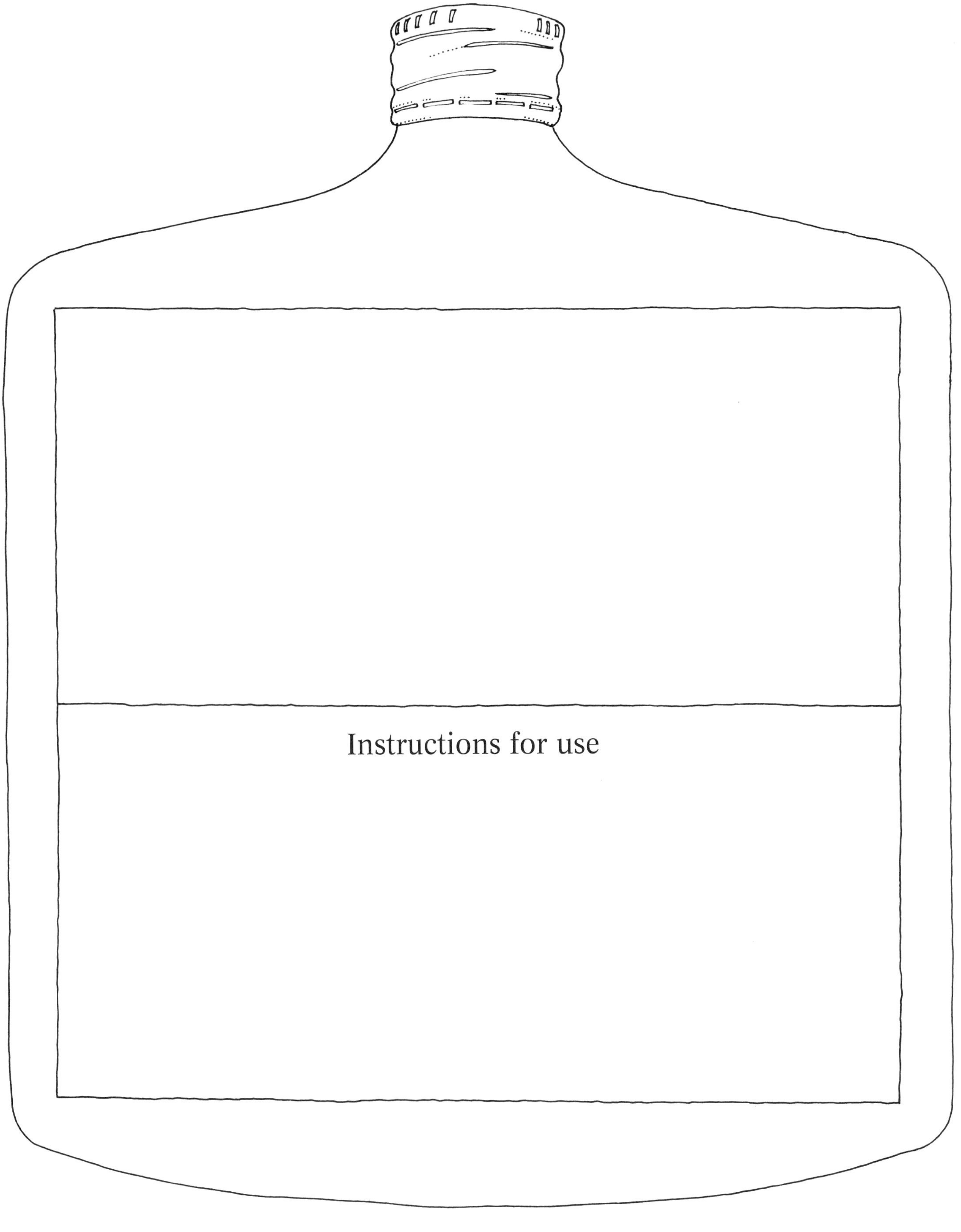

Instructions for use

The Amazing Mr Mulch

Author Rosemary Hayes

Illustrator Ian Newsham

Strand fantasy

Other Mr Mulch books

- Mr Mulch's Magic Mixtures
- The Big Shrink
- The Magic Sword

Towards Independence: C

Other books in the strand at this stage

- Mr Mulch's Magic Mixtures
- The Slippery Planet

Introducing the book

- Talk about the cover, including the title and blurb. Invite predictions about the book's contents.
- Ask the children to recall any other stories about Mr Mulch that they have read.

After reading the book

- What do the children think about Mr Mulch? What are his good and bad points? You could do a word-web for each.
- The children could be divided into pairs. One child should say why they think Mr Mulch was *right* to make the children invisible, the other why he was *wrong*. List the results under the two headings.

WORKSHEET 1
Reading Development

Activity *Finding information; sequencing events*

- Ask the children to write down in the boxes provided what Mr Mulch did to each of the people or objects on the worksheet. They will need to refer to the text.
- The children should then cut out the pictures and the boxes containing words to make cards and sequence them.
- The cards from two worksheets should be used to play a game in pairs – for example, Pairs or Snap.

Extension activity

- Ask the children to look at the writing on page 32. Can they work out what it means without using a mirror?

WORKSHEET 2
Personal Response

Activity *Ranking in order of preference*

- Ask the children to discuss which of Mr Mulch's magic tricks they liked best, giving reasons for their choice.
- The children should read the sentences that describe Mr Mulch's various tricks and cut them out. In pairs, they decide which trick was the most interesting to watch. Then they put their cut-out descriptions in order, starting with the most appealing.
- Make sure the children understand that there are a number of different rankings possible.

Extension activity

- The children could imagine that Mr Mulch is their teacher. They should write a list of magic tricks that they would like him to do.

Write what happened to each of these people or things.
Check your ideas with a friend.

Farhan	waste-bin
(page 14)	(page 16)
Oliver, Farhan, Claire	pencil
(page 15)	(page 12)
chairs	children and Mr Mulch
(page 17)	(page 18)
posters	
(page 16)	Cut these out and put them in the order in which they happened.

© CUP 1996. Original artwork by Ian Newsham.

Which of Mr Mulch's magic tricks did you enjoy most?

Cut out the boxes and put them in order, starting with the trick that you liked most.

Oliver, Claire and Farhan disappeared. They were all invisible.

Mr Mulch let go of the huge pencil and it burst into life. Everyone ducked as it roared round the classroom like a rocket.

All the chairs started to dance, jiggling about from one leg to the other.

The posters on the wall were floating round the room like magic carpets.

Farhan's hair was pink. Oliver's hair was green. Claire's hair was blue, and Sima's hair was yellow!

They found themselves rising in the air and forming a perfect pyramid.

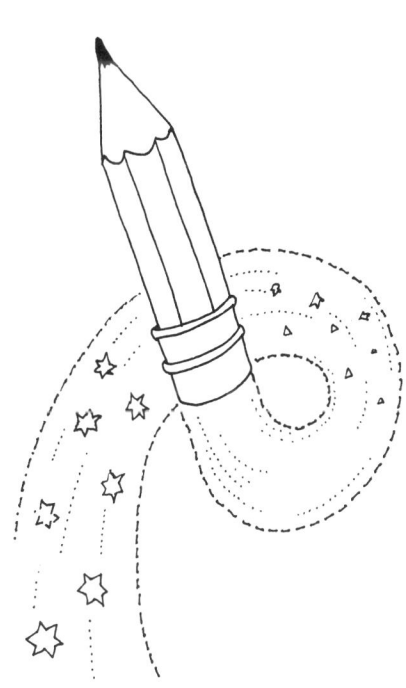

The Slippery Planet

Author Rosemary Hayes

Illustrator Ian Newsham

Strand fantasy

Towards Independence: C

Other books in the strand at this stage

- The Amazing Mr Mulch
- Mr Mulch's Magic Mixtures

Introducing the book

- Talk about the cover, including the title and blurb. Invite predictions about the book's contents.

- Ask the children if they know what the word 'planet' means. Write down their definitions of the word.

After reading the book

- Discuss books, films and TV programmes about space that the children have seen.

- Ask the children to describe the kinds of creatures that might be found in a space zoo.

WORKSHEET 1
Reading Development

Activity *Cloze; sequencing; bookmaking*

- Explain that the text on the worksheet is in the wrong order. Before they can put it in the right order, they will need to fill in the missing words.

- Ask the children to read the text, predicting the missing verbs. After filling them in, they can check their answers in the book.

Answers struggling, watched, dropped, slid, breathe, broke.

- When they have cut out and put the text in the right order, the children could make and illustrate their own small book. They will need a copy of the instructions for making a stripbook; see page 32.

WORKSHEET 2
Personal Response

Activity *Inventing a space creature*

- Look at page 4 of the book with the children. Ask them why they think the space animals look sad. Then they should look for other evidence in the story that the animals were unhappy.

- Lead the children into a discussion about why the animals were unhappy. Was it because they were in captivity, or because they were being badly treated in captivity? Extend the discussion by asking the children whether they think animals should be kept in zoos.

- Ask the children to invent an unusual space creature and to draw it on the worksheet.

- Then they should imagine that they have brought their creature to Earth for a short time. Ask them to describe in the speech bubble where they will keep it and how they will look after it. They could draw themselves next to the speech bubble.

- In pairs or small groups, the children could compare the space animals they have drawn and share their ideas about how they would care for them.

The Slippery Planet   Name _____ Date _____

These are the main events in the story. Fill in the missing words.
Cut out the boxes and put the things that happened in order.
Draw your own pictures and make a small book.

	Suddenly, the boys were _____ inside a net! And all round them were the horrible bright green people, shrieking and laughing and pointing.
	Chen and Mark _____ as the bright green skaters took the captured animal to a big, domed building made of ice.
	They _____ off the animals one by one on their own planets. Every animal said a noisy 'thank you' as it left the spaceship.
	The two boys _____ silently along the tunnel. At the end were rows of cages set into the ice. Inside the cages were lots of sad, cold, wet space animals.
	They worked all night, taking it in turns to _____ on the ice and scrape it away. Then, just as it was getting light, they _____ through the wall.

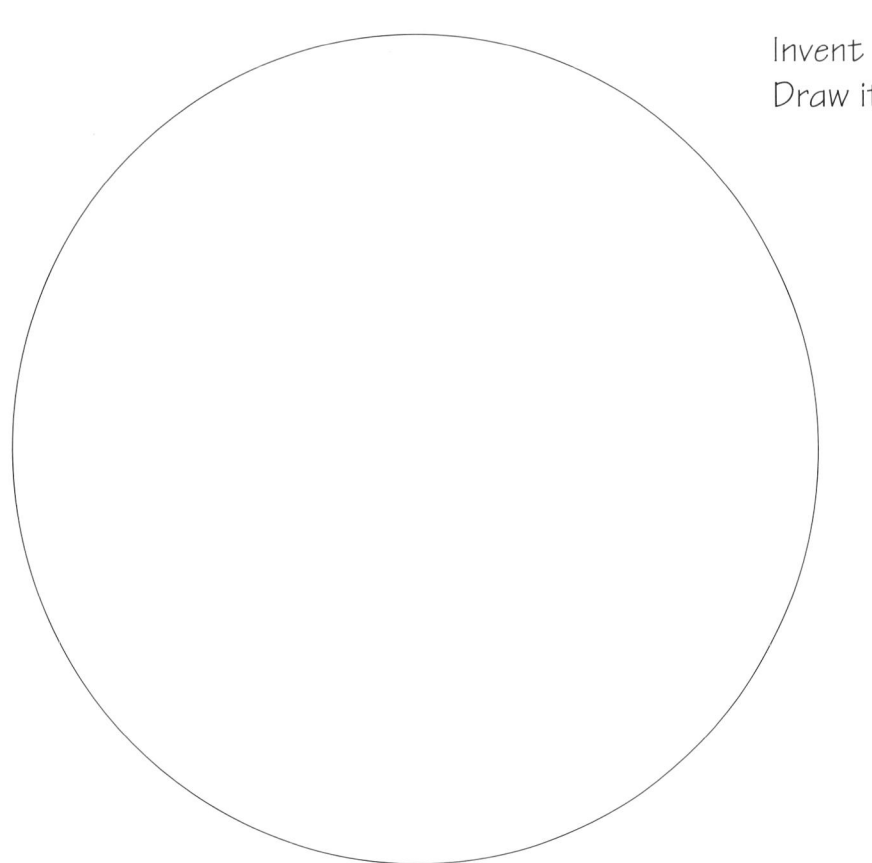

Invent an unusual space creature.
Draw it on the planet.

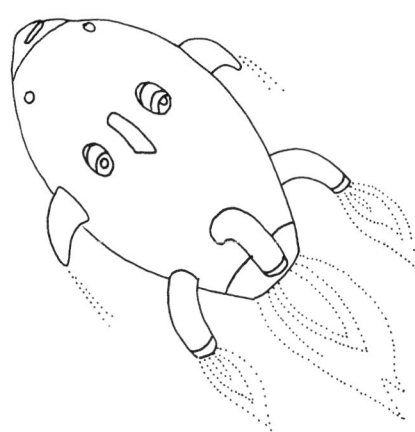

Imagine that you brought it to Earth for a short time.
Write in the speech bubble where you kept it and how you looked after it.
Then you can draw yourself.

Dancing to the River

Retold by Grace Hallworth

Illustrator Alex Ayliffe

Strand traditional tales

Other books in the strand at this stage

- How the Animals Got Their Tails
- Rabbit's Tail

Introducing the book

- Talk about the cover, including the title and blurb. Invite predictions about the book's contents.

- Explain that this story is a traditional one from the Caribbean.

After reading the book

- Ask the children whether they think the animals were right to eat the corn. Why?

- Make sure the children understand how Turtle tricked Watchman.

WORKSHEET 1
Reading Development

Activity *Comprehension: crossword*

- Talk to the children about crosswords, showing them an example. Make sure they understand the difference between 'Across' and 'Down' clues.

- Remind the children that when they fill in a crossword, they should always write one letter in each box.

- Point out that the first letter of each word is given as a clue. When they have decided on the correct words, they should trace over the first letter and then continue the word.

- Show them how to answer the first clue, referring to the book for the answer and for the correct spelling.

Answers *Across:* 3 Watchman, 5 Turtle, 8 squirrels, 9 sang. *Down:* 1 dance, 2 monkeys, 4 calypso, 6 river, 7 birds.

WORKSHEET 2
Personal Response

Activity *Writing a song*

- Read the text on the worksheet to the children and ask them to find the place it comes from in the story. Read the whole of the rhyme on page 17 aloud so that they can experience the sense of rhythm and movement it conveys.

- Ask the children to suggest other words that could be used to describe Turtle's dancing (e.g. twisted, jumped, skipped, hopped, sprang, curled, stretched). Write the words down so that the children can see them. Let them choose the ones they want to write on their worksheet.

- Invite the children, in pairs or as a group, to make up a different dancing rhyme for themselves, basing it on the rhyme in the story. They should use words they have written and words from the book.

Extension activity

- Children could perform Turtle's dance. Instructions and music are given on the next page. The music is also on page 24 of the story-book.

Turtle's Dance

Let's sing and dance to the tay-lay-lay, Let's turn and prance to the tay-lay-lay.

Hear the mu-sic play-ing And the steel pan drum-ming, As we

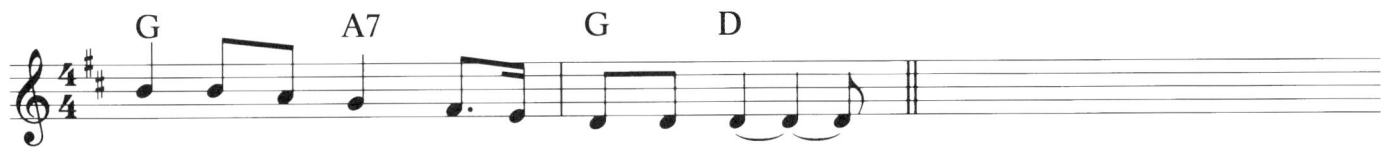

sing and we dance to the tay-lay-lay.

The children stand in two facing rows, knees slightly bent, elbows bent at right angles to body. They move as follows while singing the song through twice. All movements are made to the counts given at the end of each line.

While song is sung for the first time

Line 1 Move to right, first twisting heels at the same time, then toes at the same time. Flap hands from the wrist like fins, up and down. (4 counts – heels, toes, heels, toes)

Line 2 Repeat above, moving to left. (4 counts)

Lines 3 & 4 Rising onto toes, turn around lifting alternate feet, and end facing the other row again. Raise hands in the air, flapping them like fins. (8 counts)

Line 5 With feet still and hands on thighs, make 2 small knee bends. On last 3 notes slap thighs 3 times.

While song is sung for the second time

Lines 1 & 2 Moving forwards, and clicking their fingers in time to the music, the facing lines cross and change sides as follows. Touch floor near left heel with right toe, step forward on right foot. Touch floor near right heel with left toe, then step forward on left foot. Repeat right and left step. (8 counts.)

Lines 3, 4 & 5 As lines 3, 4 and 5 above.

The rows of children will now be facing each other as at the beginning of the dance, but on opposite sides.

Dancing to the River Name _____ Date _____

Find the answers to the clues and fill in the crossword.

Across

3. Who grabbed Turtle and put her in his bag? (page 12)
5. Who was paddling in the river? (page 7)
8. Who dug up all their hiding-places? (page 4)
9. What did Watchman do as he walked across the field? (page 13)

Down

1. What did Turtle's feet just itch to do? (page 13)
2. Who swung from tree to tree? (page 5)
4. What kind of song did Watchman sing? (page 13)
6. Where was Turtle dancing to? (page 17)
7. Who flew high above the trees? (page 3)

© CUP 1996. Original artwork by Alex Ayliffe.   Worksheet 1 Reading Development   133

She leaped and she danced.

She twirled and she pranced.

She was dancing to the river.

Write some more movement words in the water.

Make up a dancing rhyme for yourself. Write it in the box.

I _____ and I _____ .

I _____ and I _____ .

I was _____ to _____ .

What songs and music do you like best?

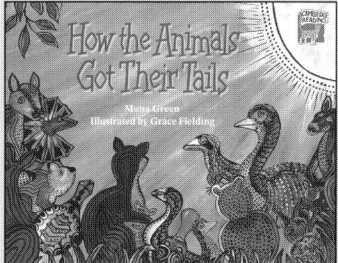

How the Animals Got Their Tails

Told by Mona Green
Edited by Pamela Lofts

Illustrator Grace Fielding

Strand traditional tales

Towards Independence: A

Other books in the strand at this stage

- Dancing to the River
- Rabbit's Tail

Introducing the book

- Talk about the cover, including the title and blurb. Invite predictions about the book's contents.

- Explain that this is a traditional tale, told by the Aboriginal people, the native inhabitants of Australia. This version was told to Pamela Lofts, who is Australian, by Mona Green, who is an Aboriginal woman. The writer has kept closely to what she was told and how she was told it.

- Tell the children the pictures have been painted by an Aboriginal artist, based on traditional dot art.

Using the book

- Be prepared for the children to meet unfamiliar words. Help them to work out what the words mean by using the context and pictures.

- Explain that a corroboree is a special meeting of Aboriginal people during which stories are told and songs and dances are performed. Sometimes it lasts for a few days and nights.

After reading the book

- Ask the children if they are familiar with other creation myths which offer an explanation about why things are as they are now. Examples are Kipling's *Just So Stories* and Joanna Troughton's picture books in Becoming a Reader C. See also *The Weather Drum* (stage B).

- The children may like to invent and illustrate their own creation myths.

WORKSHEET 1
Reading Development

Activity *Cloze; sequencing*

- Make sure the children can read all of the words they will need to choose from to complete the cloze.

- Some children may need to write the words on slips of paper first and move them around the cloze to find the right places for them. Then they can copy the answers in.

- Once they have finished, they can check their answers by looking at pages 8 and 9 of the book.

- For the drawing and writing task, ask the children to concentrate on the next important or dramatic point in the story. They will need to refer back to the book to help them choose this.

WORKSHEET 2
Personal Response

Activity *Inventing an animal; word play*

- Ask the children to look at the pictures of animals with the tails they originally had (page 4). See if they can identify each animal.

- Discuss the task on the worksheet. Explain that the children can choose tails that make very strange animals if they like.

- Introduce the idea of making a new word by combining existing words.

Extension activities

- Make a list of animals and encourage the children to suggest new animals by combining different features of two animals (e.g. a 'tiraffe' could be a long-necked tiger, a 'crocaroo' could be a bouncing crocodile).

- The children could make a class book of new animals, drawing and labelling each one.

How the Animals Got Their Tails   Name _____

Use these words to fill in the gaps.

branches   dancing   hung   tails

over   hanging   low   ground

They took off their tails! Then they _____ them
up in the _____ of a tree, some high, some
_____ , all _____ the tree. They didn't
want to leave them just lying on the _____ .
   That tree was full of _____ . The animals just
left them _____ there while they went off to join
in the singing and _____ .

Draw and write about what happened next in the story.

Draw here.	Write here.

© CUP 1996. Original artwork by Grace Fielding.

How the Animals Got Their Tails

Name _____

Copy a tail from the tail tree onto each of the animals.
Choose tails that will make interesting new animals.

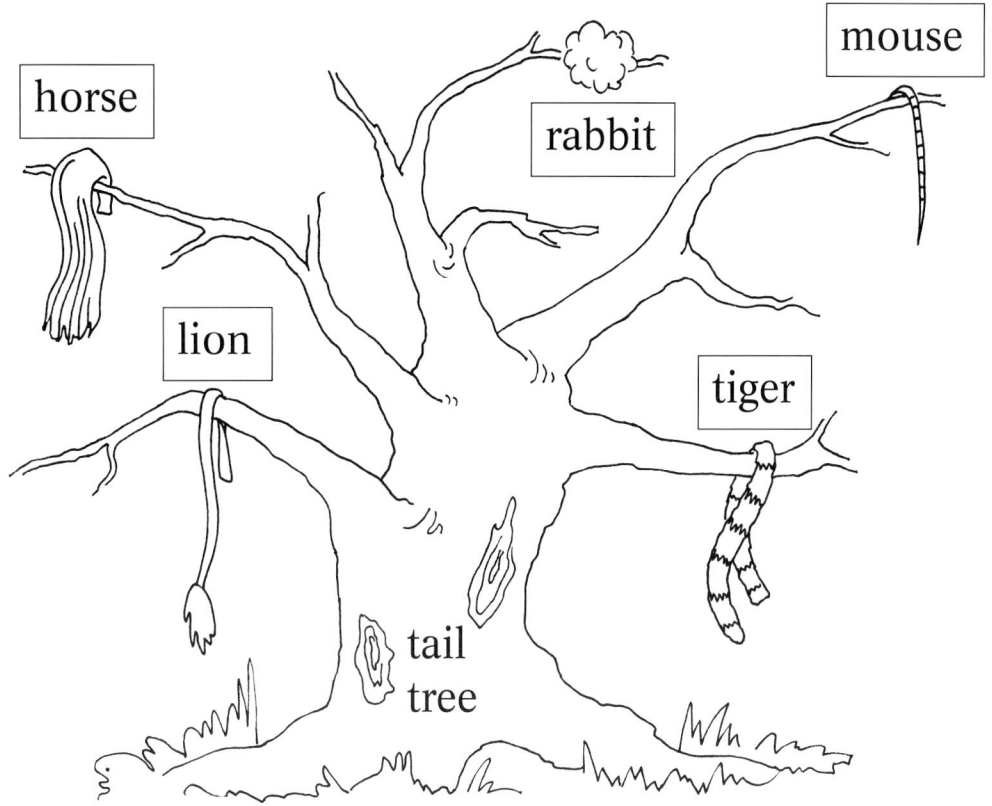

horse

rabbit

mouse

lion

tiger

tail
tree

Give each new animal a new name by mixing up the old animals' names.
For example, tiger + dog = tidog.

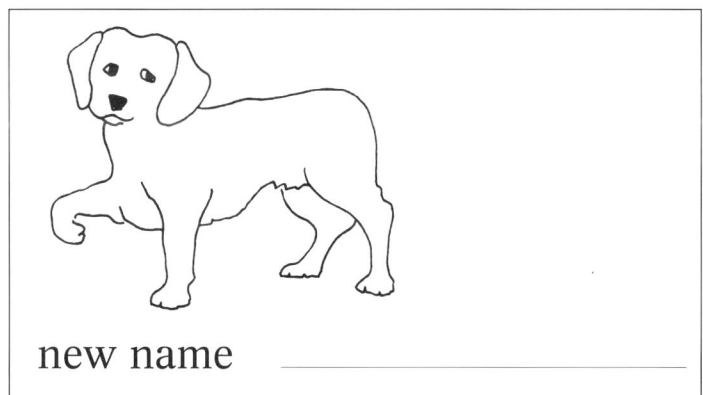

new name _____

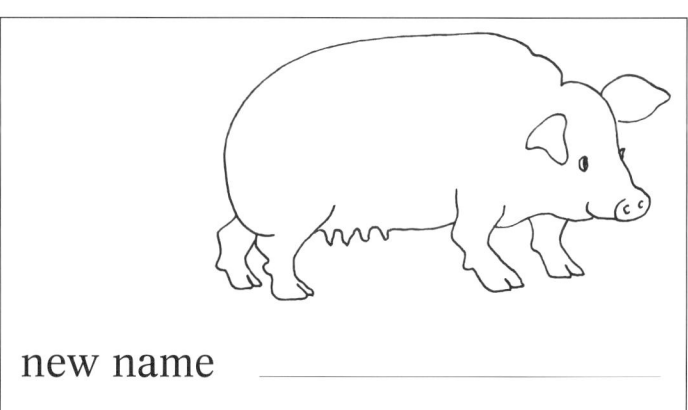

new name _____

new name _____

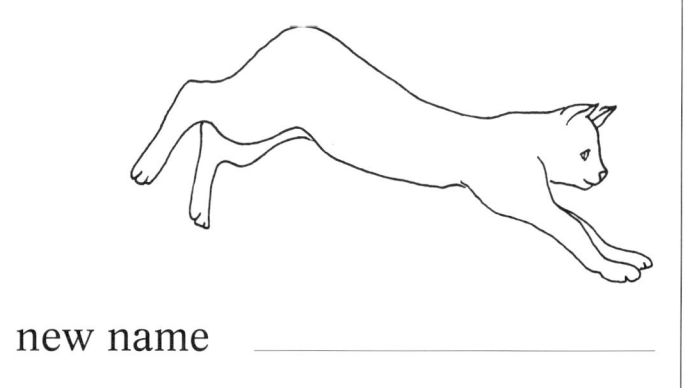

new name _____

Worksheet 2 Personal Response 137

Rabbit's Tail

Retold by Duncan Williamson
and Linda Williamson

Illustrator David Parkins

Strand traditional tales

Towards Independence: A

Other books in the strand at this stage

- Dancing to the River
- How the Animals Got Their Tails

Introducing the book

- Talk about the cover, including the title and blurb. Invite predictions about the book's contents.
- Explain that this is a traditional story that comes from Scotland.

After reading the book

- Identify who the main characters in the story are and ask the children to describe them.
- Consider the character of Jack Frost. Have the children come across him in other stories? Which ones?
- Discuss what is meant by boasting. Ask the children to think of examples.
- Talk about whether Fox was right to trick Rabbit, and whether the other animals were right to tell Fox that Rabbit was boasting.

WORKSHEET 1
Reading Development

Activity *Classification: descriptions*

- Ask the children to read the descriptions of characters on the worksheet. Discuss who each might be. They can use the text to help them and to check their ideas.
- The children should write the appropriate description next to the picture of each character.

Extension activity

- Ask each child to think of a well-known character from a story (e.g. Cinderella, Goldilocks) or a recurring figure (e.g. giant, witch, wolf).
- The children should write down two or three things about this character without mentioning who or what they are. Then they read out what they have written to a partner. Their partner tries to work out who the mystery character is.

WORKSHEET 2
Personal Response

Activity *Problem solving*

- Discuss how Rabbit's appearance changed during the story. Do the children prefer the way he looked before or after Stork rescued him?
- Ask the children to think of a way in which Stork could have rescued Rabbit without any of his features being changed.
- Before they start the worksheet, encourage the children to talk about how they would have rescued Rabbit. What rescue equipment would they have needed?
- The children then write about the method they would use and draw a picture of what they would do.

Rabbit's Tail

Name _____ Date _____

Write the descriptions next to the right character.

the wisest creature of all   long legs and long beak

two big ears and a little, short tail

long, spiky nose and spiky fingers   long, bushy tail

Rabbit's Tail

Name _____   Date _____

You must help me! My beautiful tail is caught in the ice.

If you had come along instead of Stork, how would you have rescued Rabbit?
Draw and write about your idea.

Draw here.

Write here.

The Lord Mount Dragon

Retold by Keith Ruttle

Illustrator Rowan Barnes-Murphy

Strand traditional tales

Other books in the strand at this stage
- The Weather Drum
- Volcano Woman

Introducing the book

- Talk about the cover, including the title and blurb. Invite predictions about the book's contents.
- Explain that this is a traditional story from Ireland, and that variations of the story are told in many other countries.

After reading the book

- Ask the children to contrast the weaver's view of himself with the way the people saw him (e.g. wearing suit of armour/saucepans).
- What do the children think of the weaver and the king? Was the weaver foolish or brave? Was the king cruel to send the weaver to find the dragon?
- Discuss the ending of the story. Do the children think everyone got the reward they deserved?

WORKSHEET 1
Reading Development

Activity *Exploring a character's emotions*

- Look through the book with the children, stopping to ask them how they think the weaver felt at different points. Make a list of the words the children use, and of new words you introduce them to, so that they can read them.
- Let the children use these words to complete the sentences on the worksheet, encouraging them to use more than one word to describe each emotion. Do the first one with the children as an example (e.g. 'Early in the morning I felt exhausted and hungry.').
- Ask the children to compare their answers.

WORKSHEET 2
Personal Response

Activity *Ranking events*

- Ask the children which part of the story they liked best. There will probably be a variety of responses.
- Seven high points in the story are set out on the worksheet. Use these to refer the children back to these points in the book. Ask what they felt and thought at each point.
- The children should then rank three of the boxes, starting with their favourite part. They should explain their choice to a partner.
- Make it clear that there are several possible rankings.

Extension activity

- The children could use the boxes to retell the story orally and/or in writing.

The Lord Mount Dragon Name _____

How did the weaver feel in different parts of the story?

Finish the sentences.

Early in the morning I felt

_____

_____ .

When I saw my porridge covered

in flies, I felt _____

_____ .

When the dragon roared into the

sky, I felt _____

_____ .

When the dragon stunned itself,

I felt _____

_____ .

At the end of the story I felt

_____

_____ .

The Lord Mount Dragon

Name _____

Cut out the boxes and put them in order, starting with the part that you liked best.

Here are some of the most exciting points of the story. Which three did you like best?

(page 4) The weaver kills seventy with one blow.	(pages 7–9) The weaver makes himself some armour out of pots and pans.
(pages 14–16) The weaver meets the king, who is planning a cruel trick.	(page 19) The horse gallops straight to the dragon's swamp.
(pages 20–21) The weaver meets the terrifying dragon.	(page 23) The weaver clings to the dragon's ear.
(pages 30–31) The weaver rides into the village with the king.	

The Weather Drum

Retold by Rosalind Kerven

Illustrator Vladyana Krykorka

Strand traditional tales

Towards Independence: B

Other books in the strand at this stage

• The Lord Mount Dragon

• Volcano Woman

Introducing the book

• Talk about the cover, including the title and blurb. Invite predictions about the book's contents.

• Explain that this story is a traditional tale from Siberia. Read the last page of the book with the children to give them some information about the people who told the story.

After reading the book

• Ask the children why the storm made the people in the village miserable.

• Ask the children to explain how Big Raven tricked Universe and Rain Woman.

• Ask the children if they are familiar with other creation myths which offer an explanation about why things are as they are now. Examples are Kipling's *Just So Stories* and Joanna Troughton's picture books in Becoming a Reader C. See also *How the Animals Got Their Tails* (stage A).

WORKSHEET 1
Reading Development

Activity *Sequencing; bookmaking*

• Ask the children to cut up the strips of the story, then put them in the right order and number them.

• The children should use the strips to create a small book. They could illustrate this and take it home to share with their family and friends. See page 32 of this book.

Extension activity

• You or a child could take the role of Universe. Using the technique of hot-seating, the children then question this character about his motives and powers.

WORKSHEET 2
Personal Response

Activity *Extension of ideas*

• Refer the children to the points in the story when Big Raven's magic powers are introduced. Talk about the ones featured on the worksheet (these can be found on pages 4–5, 14 and 20).

• Ask the children to share their ideas about what they would do if they had Big Raven's magic powers.

• Invite the children to draw a magic costume and to tell a partner what magic powers it has. They should then write down a description of the costume and explain what they would change into and the spell they would cast.

Extension activity

• The children could use the ideas on their worksheet as a basis for writing a story.

The Weather Drum

Name _____ Date _____

Cut out the strips and put them in the right order.
Make a small book. Draw your own pictures.

So Big Raven changed into a tiny piece of reindeer fur and hid in the tent. He wanted to stop them drumming.

Long ago, there was a terrible storm. Everyone was soaked through and icy cold.

Now, with every drum-beat the weather turned fine. Everyone was happy.

Big Raven flew to the Sky World. He could hear a dreadful noise coming from a big tent.

Big Raven held the magic drum and stick over the fire. The storm-making powers turned into sunshine-making powers.

He made a sleep-spell and sent Universe and Rain Woman to sleep.

Inside the tent were the Great Chief Universe and his wife Rain Woman. They did not stop drumming.

Universe and Rain Woman woke up and banged on the drum again.

Big Raven had powerful magic.

He could fly in a magic costume.

He could change into a tiny
piece of reindeer fur.

He could cast a sleep-spell.

If you had Big Raven's magic, what would you do with it?

Draw your magic costume here.	What would you change into?
	What spell would you cast?

Volcano Woman

Retold by Rosalind Kerven

Illustrator Chris Molan

Strand traditional tales

Towards Independence: B

Other books in the strand at this stage
- The Lord Mount Dragon
- The Weather Drum

Introducing the book

- Talk about the cover, including the title and blurb. Invite predictions about the book's contents.

- Explain that this is a traditional story from Hawaii. Read the explanation at the back of the book about the people who told the story.

After reading the book

- How would the children describe the atmosphere at the party?

- Ask the children what they think about the way Kaha-wali was driven from the island.

- Discuss how the volcano and earthquake are similar to Pele's anger.

- Point out the variety of words in the story that mean 'said'. Ask the children to suggest why the author might have chosen to use them.

WORKSHEET 1
Reading Development

Activity *Completing descriptions; drawing*

- Read the incomplete clauses and sentences on the worksheet with the children and see if they can suggest what the missing words might be.

- They can then compare their ideas with the author's by referring to the relevant pages.

- The children can either copy the words, or try to write from memory.

Answers *Left:* lightning; glowed; thunder. *Right:* hot wind; crackled; dancing, yellow flames.

Extension activity

- You or a child could take the role of Kaha-wali. Using the technique of hot-seating, the children then question this character about what happened after he left the island and how he found another home.

WORKSHEET 2
Personal Response

Activity *Relating text to personal experience*

- Pele's nature is fiery and angry. It provides the impetus for the story. Discuss what anger is and what makes us angry. Ask the children to help you draw up a list of things that make them angry and encourage a few of them to tell the stories behind their answers.

- Explain that the children should focus on one occasion when they were angry. The worksheet is split up into three parts: the cause of the anger, what happened and how the anger was overcome. They should write about their experience in the three spaces, and draw pictures of the events.

- If some of the children cannot recall a time when they were angry, they might be able to think of a character in a book or on television who became angry, and pretend to be that character.

Extension activity

- The children could use the same framework to explore other emotions (e.g. sadness, excitement, worry).

How does the writer describe Pele?

_____
sparkled from
her fingertips.
(page 20)

Pele was like a
_____ .
(page 20)

Draw a picture of Pele here.

Her eyes
_____ .
(page 14)

Her hair
_____ .
(page 14)

She roared like
_____ .
(page 20)

Her whole body
seemed to turn into
_____ .
(page 20)

Volcano Woman   Name _____   Date _____

The proud goddess Pele was very angry when she was
woken up and Kaha-wali beat her in the sledge race.

We all feel angry at times.
Write about and draw what happened when you were really angry.

I became angry because	
So I	
I didn't calm down until	

Coyote Girl

Retold by Rosalind Kerven

Illustrator Amanda Hall

Strand traditional tales

Towards Independence: C

Other books in the strand at this stage

- The Cape of Rushes
- The Most Beautiful Child

Introducing the book

- Talk about the cover, including the title and blurb. Invite predictions about the book's contents.

- Explain that this is a traditional story told by the Hopi people. Read pages 31 and 32 with the children to find out about them.

After reading the book

- Ask the children what things they like about their friends. Do they think Blue Corn Maiden and Yellow Corn Maiden were good friends? Why?

- Discuss the message of the story, on page 30. Do the children think that Grandmother Spider was right? Why?

- Ask the children what they think about Yellow Corn Maiden's punishment.

WORKSHEET 1
Reading Development

Activity *Comprehension and classification*

- Divide the children into pairs. Ask one child in each pair to make up statements about characters in the book. Then the other child should try to guess which characters their partner's statements are about.

- The children should read through the questions on the worksheet. Before they start the activity, ask if they can tell you whether each one comes from the beginning, middle or end of the story.

- Do the first question with the children.

Answers 1 Red, 2 Yellow, 3 Blue, 4 Yellow, 5 Black, 6 Black, 7 Yellow, 8 Blue, 9 Black.

Extension activity

- Ask the children to suggest positive statements about other members of the class.

WORKSHEET 2
Personal Response

Activity *Ranking events*

- Discuss with the children the idea of revenge – 'an eye for an eye, a tooth for a tooth' and so on.

- Ask the children to read the passages on the worksheet, then to find each one in the book so that they can place it in its context.

- In pairs they should cut the passages out and decide how to rank them.

- Make sure the children understand that this is an open-ended task – there are a number of possible rankings.

Coyote Girl Name _____ Date _____

Answer these questions by underlining them
in the right colour for the character.

| Yellow Corn Maiden | Blue Corn Maiden, the coyote girl | A hunter | Spider Woman |
| yellow | blue | red | black |

1. Who picked up his bow and arrows? (page 16)

2. Who thought about how angry she was? (page 4)

3. Who was gentle and sweet? (page 2)

4. Who pulled something strange and beautiful out of her dress? (page 6)

5. Who was an old old woman? (page 20)

6. Who hung the pot over her fire? (page 23)

7. Who was cross and spiteful? (page 2)

8. Who could run as fast as the wind? (page 12)

9. Who sent a group of dancers to show the coyote girl her way? (page 26)

Lots of bad things happened to the two girls. Which is the most frightening? With a partner, put them in order, starting with the worst.

But one day they argued too much.

"I hate you, I hate you!" screamed Yellow Corn Maiden in a rage.

And at last she understood. Yellow Corn Maiden's magic rainbow wheel had turned her into a wild dog, a coyote!

The coyote girl pushed open the door and went in. She could smell rabbit meat, left behind by the hunters.

She found the meat and gobbled it up.

The hunters tied up the coyote girl's paws so that she could not escape.

"Let me see that!" cried Yellow Corn Maiden. She snatched it away rudely. Then she drank from it – and, at once, Spider Woman turned her into a snake!

The Cape of Rushes

Retold by Antonia Barber

Illustrator Amanda Harvey

Strand traditional tales

Towards Independence: C

Other books in the strand at this stage

- Coyote Girl
- The Most Beautiful Child

Introducing the book

- Talk about the cover, including the title and blurb. Invite predictions about the book's contents.
- Explain that this is a traditional story from Britain.
- Prepare the children to accept that the vocabulary and language structures used in this book are challenging.
- Read the first page with the children and then stop. Ask whether they think the king's question to his daughters could cause problems. What problems could there be?

After reading the book

- Discuss the statements made by each daughter and the reaction of their father to each.
- Discuss the author's use of language and vocabulary. Can the children recognise why the author has used archaic language?

WORKSHEET 1
Reading Development

Activity *Finding synonyms*

- Tell the children to cover or fold under the words in the rushes at the bottom of the worksheet. Ask them to read the passage on the worksheet. Can they tell which part of the story it comes from? What clues are they using? Help them to find the passage (on page 8).
- Re-read the passage with the children, asking them to suggest words which mean the same as the underlined words.
- Ask the children to look at the words in the rushes and decide which of them is closest in meaning to each of the underlined words.
- When they have completed the worksheet, discuss why the author chose to use the underlined words.

Extension activity

- Working in groups, the children could create their own dictionary of synonyms for this book by finding unfamiliar words and suggesting alternatives.

WORKSHEET 2
Personal Response

Activity *Relating text to personal experience*

- Ask the children who or what they love the most. Accept answers such as 'football' as well as others. They should say why they made their choice.
- Explain that they should write down the person or thing they love the most. While they are drawing themselves in the centre, they can be thinking about what to write in the speech bubbles.

The Cape of Rushes Name _____ Date _____

Find this passage in the book.

> Alone in the dark night, she shivered in her <u>fine</u> silk dress until the rising moon showed that her path was <u>fringed</u> with beds of rushes. These she <u>gathered</u> as she went and, with <u>nimble</u> fingers, wove a long cape to cover her dress from top to toe.
>
> It was as well that she did, for soon the rain began to fall. Her lovely hair grew <u>bedraggled</u> and her <u>dainty</u> shoes grew muddy, but, beneath the cape of rushes, her white dress stayed clean and dry.

Write the word or words that is closest in meaning to the underlined words.

1. _____ is close in meaning to <u>fine</u>.

2. _____ means nearly the same as <u>fringed</u>.

3. _____ is close in meaning to <u>nimble</u>.

4. _____ is close in meaning to <u>gathered</u>.

5. _____ means nearly the same as <u>bedraggled</u>.

6. _____ is close in meaning to <u>dainty</u>.

Use these words.

untidy   quick   beautiful   picked   edged   small and delicate

The Cape of Rushes   Name _____   Date _____

I love you as I love my life!

I love you more than anything in the world!

Who, or what, do you love most? _____

Draw yourself in the centre below. Fill in the speech bubbles to explain your love.

I love _____
as much as

I love _____
more than

I love _____
when

I love _____
because

The Most Beautiful Child

Retold by Debjani Chatterjee

Strand traditional tales

Other books in the strand at this stage

- Coyote Girl
- The Cape of Rushes

Introducing the book

- Talk about the cover, including the title and blurb. Invite predictions about the book's contents.
- Explain that this is a traditional story from India.
- Make sure that the children know Lakshmi is the Hindu goddess of good luck and beauty.

After reading the book

- Ask the children to brainstorm what they regard as beautiful. Discuss the range and variety of things that could come into that category.

WORKSHEET 1
Reading Development

Activity *Bookmaking and illustrating*

- Give each child a photocopy of the bookmaking activity on page 31.
- Part of the story is re-created on the worksheet. The children should follow the instructions to make the booklet and illustrate it appropriately. This could then be taken home and read.

WORKSHEET 2
Personal Response

Activity *Relating text to personal experience*

- Ask the children why the owl thought her own baby was the most beautiful child. If the children do not recall this, draw their attention to the statement 'In every mother's eyes, her own child is the most beautiful of all!'
- The children should imagine that they have a precious gift to give to a very special person. Working in small groups, they should talk about what kind of present would be special, and who they would give it to.
- They should then draw their special person with the present in the box on the worksheet, and write some sentences about their choice alongside.

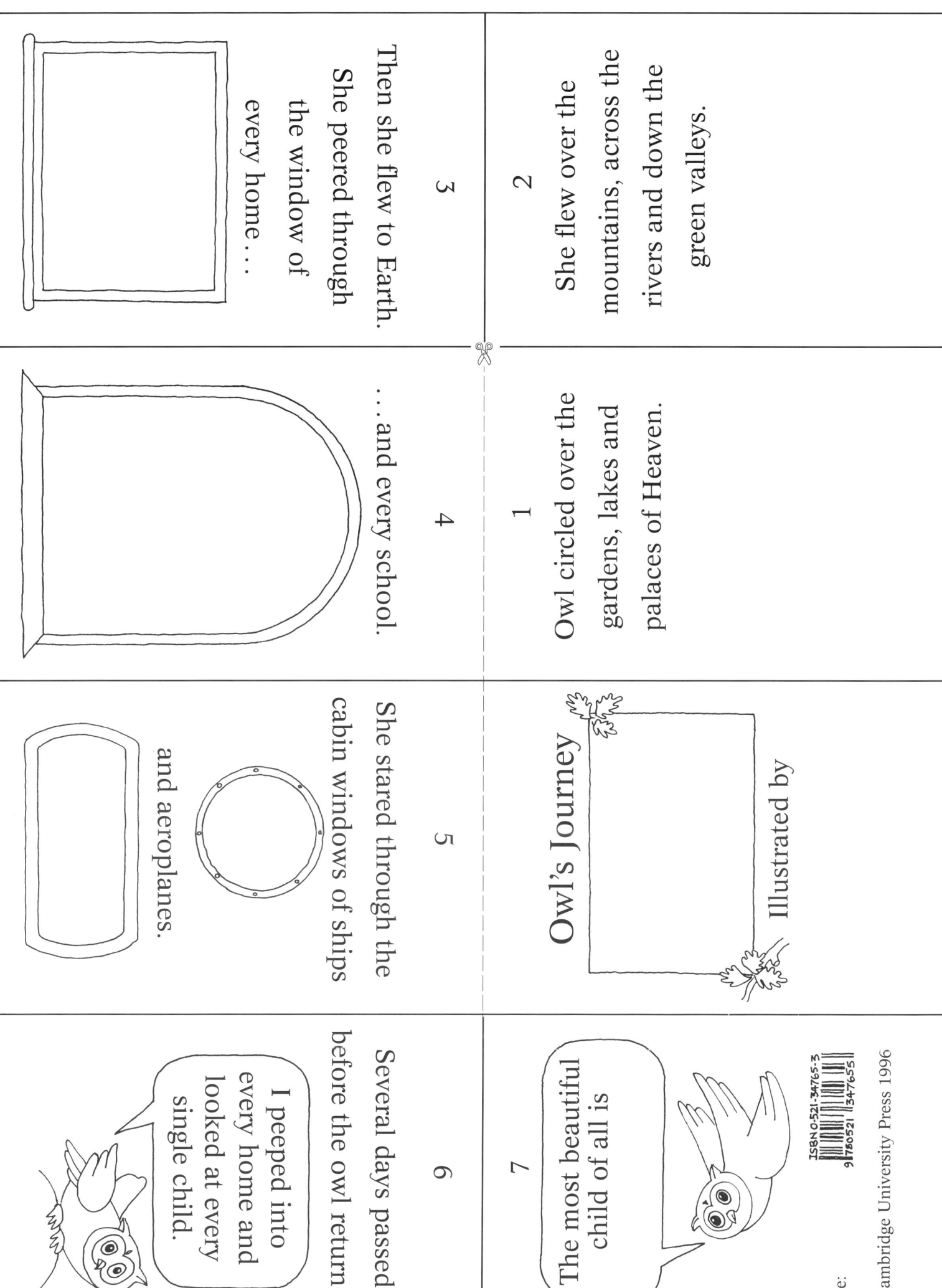

3

Then she flew to Earth. She peered through the window of every home …

2

She flew over the mountains, across the rivers and down the green valleys.

4

…and every school.

1

Owl circled over the gardens, lakes and palaces of Heaven.

5

She stared through the cabin windows of ships and aeroplanes.

Owl's Journey

Illustrated by

6

Several days passed before the owl returned.

7

The most beautiful child of all is

I peeped into every home and looked at every single child.

ISBN 0-521-34765-3

Price:

© Cambridge University Press 1996

The Most Beautiful Child   Name _____

If you had a wonderful present to give to a special person,
who would you give it to?

I would like to give this necklace
to someone very special.

Draw your special person with the present.

Write about why you chose that person.

Ben's Amazing Birthday

Author Richard Brown

Illustrator Annabel Large

Strand stories of childhood

Towards Independence: A

Other books in the strand at this stage

• Dad's Promise

• Tulips for Dad

Introducing the book

• Talk about the cover, including the title and blurb. Invite predictions about the book's contents.

• Point to the picture of Ben Robinson-Young on the inside back cover and explain that the story is a true account of what happened on his sixth birthday, in 1994.

• Ask a child to point out Australia on a map. Make it clear that Ben was on holiday there.

• Ask the children to guess what a bushfire is.

After reading the book

• To develop the birthday theme, encourage some of the children to talk about any particular birthday that they remember.

WORKSHEET 1
Reading Development

Activity   *Cloze: vocabulary extension*

• Ask the children to read the sentences and to predict what the missing words could be before they write their answers.

• Some children may need to write the words on slips of paper first and move them around on the cloze to find the right places for them. Then they can copy the answers in.

• After writing down their answers, they should check them in the book.

• The children should choose a sentence from the book to make their own cloze sentence for a friend to complete.

WORKSHEET 2
Personal Response

Activity   *Writing a report*

• Read the speech bubbles at the top of the work-sheet. Then, with the help of the children, recap on what happened to Ben on his birthday.

• Ask the children if they remember a really special birthday. If not, do they remember any other exciting day? They could share some of their stories before filling in the worksheet.

• Point out the three picture boxes, which will help them focus on the beginning, middle and end of their picture story.

Extension activity

• The pictures could be used as prompts for story-telling in pairs.

Ben's Amazing Birthday

Name _____

Use these words to complete the sentences.

skin   hair   radio   down   grey   burning   trees   dark

Dust and ash floated down onto our _____ and _____ .
(page 10)

Then the _____ went silent.   (page 6)

Flames crackled in the _____ .   (page 4)

Homes were burnt _____ and people had to flee.   (page 4)

Thick clouds of _____ smoke hung in the sky and the air smelt of _____ .
(page 10)

Smoke turned the sky _____ .   (page 4)

Add your own sentence for a friend to complete.

Ben's Amazing Birthday   Name _____

What an amazing day it's been.

You won't forget this birthday party, will you?

Have you had a special day that you won't forget?
Draw what happened, and write a caption below each picture.

First

Then

Finally

Why was it special for you?

Dad's Promise

Author Richard Brown

Illustrator Anthony Lewis

Strand stories of childhood

Towards Independence: A

Other books in the strand at this stage

- Ben's Amazing Birthday
- Tulips for Dad

Introducing the book

- Talk about the cover, including the title and blurb. Invite predictions about the book's contents.
- Check the children understand that this is a true story. It happened to Kate Ruttle in Edinburgh in about 1970.

After reading the book

- Have any children ever got lost? Invite some personal stories.
- Ask the children what they should do if they do get lost.

WORKSHEET 1
Reading Development

Activity *Classification: vocabulary extension*

- Discuss what Kate felt about the people and situations on the worksheet.
- Help the children to read and then talk about the words they can choose from.
- Encourage them to add words of their own.
- The children can draw the policeman in the space provided.

WORKSHEET 2
Personal Response

Activity *Relating text to personal experience*

- Refer the children to the picture on pages 8–9, and read the whole passage again to them.
- Ask the children to read aloud the quotation on the worksheet.
- Have any children experienced a broken promise? Encourage personal storytelling about promises.
- Explain how to complete the worksheet. If any child has no story of their own about a promise, suggest they invent one.
- Talk about whether the promise made to them was kept.

Dad's Promise   Name _____   Date _____

What did Kate feel about each of these situations or people?
Add your own words to the list, then choose words from the list to write in the boxes below.
Draw your own picture of the policeman.

frightened	scared
sad	tired
relieved	unhappy
happy	
safe	
worried	
cold	

The ballet teacher

Kate felt

Walking home and getting lost

Kate felt

Meeting the policeman

Kate felt

Dad's Promise

Name _____ Date _____

"Do you promise?" I asked.

"I promise," said Dad.

"Every time?" I asked.

"Every time," promised Dad. (page 9)

Has someone ever promised you something? Draw who made the promise, and write the promise in the speech bubble.

Was the promise kept? _____

Have you ever made a promise? What happened?

Tulips for Dad

Author Richard Brown

Illustrator Cliff Wright

Strand stories of childhood

Towards Independence: A

Other books in the strand at this stage

- Ben's Amazing Birthday
- Dad's Promise

Introducing the book

- Talk about the cover, including the title and blurb. Invite predictions about the book's contents.

- Explain that this is a story told to the writer by Margaret Smith, who is remembering an event in her childhood. Show the children the photo on the inside back cover.

- Point out to the children that the events in the story happened in the 1940s.

After reading the book

- Ask the children why we take flowers to someone who is ill.

- What do the children think Dad was feeling at the end of the story? What did the neighbour think about Margaret?

WORKSHEET 1
Reading Development

Activity *Comprehension: crossword*

- Show the children examples of crosswords in newspapers and discuss why they think people enjoy doing these.

- Check that the children understand the 'Across' and 'Down' conventions of crosswords.

- Point out that the first letter of each word is given as a clue. The children should trace over the first letter and then continue the word.

Answers *Across:* 4 wheelbarrow, 6 garden.
Down: 1 flowers, 2 shears, 3 trowel, 5 weeds.

Extension activity

- Ask the children to make a list of their friends and relatives, or of characters in books they have read recently. Suggest that they use these names to create a crossword of names.

WORKSHEET 2
Personal Response

Activity *Alternative plot lines*

- Ask the children to think of a time when someone they knew was ill. Encourage them to talk about it. Lead the discussion into what the children can do to help when a parent is not feeling well.

- Pointing to the worksheet, ask the children why Margaret's mum wasn't pleased about the tulip heads.

- Share ideas about what else Margaret could have done.

- The children should draw and write about one of their ideas in the boxes provided, or draw one and write about another.

Tulips for Dad Name _____ Date _____

Complete the crossword.
Use the clues below

Across

4. This was made for Margaret. (page 2)

6. A place Margaret 'messed about' in. (page 3)

Down

1. Margaret wanted to give some of these to her dad. (page 17)

2. This tool went 'snip-snip' in the story. (page 2)

3. Margaret used this to dig holes. (page 3)

5. You don't want these in your garden. (page 4)

Tulips for Dad   Name_____   Date_____

Margaret said,

> I've brought some flowers for Daddy.
> They're to help him get better.

But her mum didn't seem at all pleased.

What else could Margaret have done to make her dad feel better?
Draw and write your answers in the boxes.

Write here.

Draw here.

A Welsh Lamb

Author Richard Brown

Illustrator Patricia Ludlow

Strand stories of childhood

Towards Independence: B

Other books in the strand at this stage
- Dancing in Soot
- The Haystack

Introducing the book

- Talk about the cover, including the title and blurb. Invite predictions about the book's contents.

- Explain that this story was told to the author by Martin Williams, who was about six when it happened to him. The setting is Wales in 1955. Show the children the pictures on the inside back cover.

After reading the book

- Encourage two or three children to talk about their pets, especially any unusual ones.

- Ask the children to compare the dog's and the lamb's suitability as pets. Check that they understand why the lamb had to be released.

WORKSHEET 1
Reading Development

Activity *Cloze; matching pictures and text*

- Ask the children to read the statements at the bottom of the sheet. If necessary, help them to find the first missing word.

- When they have completed the activity, encourage the children to use the page numbers to check their answers in the book.

WORKSHEET 2
Personal Response

Activity *Relating text to personal experience*

- Show the children the picture on page 7 and read the text below it aloud.

- Discuss the possibility of finding a living creature in the wild (i.e. that does not appear to have an owner) which could be kept as a pet for a while. Make sure the children understand that this should not be someone else's pet or property. Draw up a list of such creatures.

- In the discussion, use the leopard's question as a focus.

- Before the children draw and write on the worksheet, explain that their picture should show where the creature was found as well as the creature itself. They could refer to reference books for help with their pictures.

Use the words to fill in the boxes.
Cut out the boxes and match them to the pictures.

stayed   wagged   feel   shivered

Finding the lamb.	
Keith carries the lamb home.	
Judy meets the lamb.	
Letting Snowy go.	

I knew that Snowy was where he belonged, and that made me _____ better. (page 32)	It _____ as I touched it. Perhaps it was afraid of me. (page 7)
It wriggled a bit at first, then it _____ still. (page 10)	At first, she growled. Then she sniffed the lamb. Judy _____ her tail. (page 14)

© CUP 1996. Original artwork by Patricia Ludlow.

A Welsh Lamb Name _____ Date _____

Then I was alone with the lamb.

It shivered as I touched it.

Perhaps it was afraid of me.

   I wanted to keep the lamb as

a pet. (page 7)

What creature would you like to find?

I would like to have it as a pet
because

What problems might
you have with it?

---

170   Worksheet 2 Personal Response   © CUP 1996. Original artwork by Patricia Ludlow.

Dancing in Soot

Author Richard Brown

Illustrator Patrice Aggs

Strand stories of childhood

Towards Independence: B

Other books in the strand at this stage

- A Welsh Lamb
- The Haystack

Introducing the book

- Talk about the cover, including the title and blurb. Invite predictions about the book's contents.

- Point to the picture of the children on the cover and explain that this is a true story about them, which happened in 1955, and that it is told by the girl, who is now an adult called Deirdre MacArthur-George. Show the picture on the inside back cover.

After reading the book

- To develop one of the themes of the book, ask the children to try to remember a time when they got very messy and to think about their family's reaction. Invite some of the children to tell their stories.

- Turn back to pages 2 and 3, showing the farm where the children played, and ask the children the following questions: What makes it a good play area? What sort of play area would they like to have?

WORKSHEET 1
Reading Development

Activity *Cloze: vocabulary extension*

- After reading pages 15–17, ask the children to read through the part of the story on the worksheet. Encourage them to predict as they read the words that might fit in the spaces.

- Do the first few words with them to model the activity.

- Some children could cover the list of words at the top of the worksheet and try to write the words independently. Others may need to write the words on slips of paper first and move them around on the cloze to find the right places for them. They can then copy the answers in.

- Introduce the children to the study skill of ticking off words from a list as they use the words on the worksheet.

- Make sure the children check their answers in the book.

WORKSHEET 2
Personal Response

Activity *Writing reports*

- Ask the children what differences there are between thinking and speaking.

- Make sure the children understand the convention of the thought bubble, which is usually drawn with a wavy edge and has dots or circles linking it with the person who is thinking.

- Talk about the worksheet. Before they begin work on their own, help the children to find pages on which the characters appear. Ask the children to role-play being Mum. What does she think? Then ask them to role-play what each of the other characters think. Concentrate on key words (e.g. fun, naughty, messy, silly, fair, thoughtless).

Read pages 15 to 17. Shut the book and try to fill in the missing words.

noises   faces   burst   dance   fingers

sack   lives   flour   toes   clowns

There was a pile of sacks. Some of the sacks had _____ and were spilling soot onto the yard. We poked our _____ into it. It was black, and it felt like _____ .

David wiped his fingers on the _____ , and this gave us an idea. We smeared soot on our arms and _____ . We pretended to be _____ .

Then I stuck my _____ into the soot and did a wild little _____ , waving my arms about and making funny _____ . David joined in, and the soot flew around. We had the time of our _____ .

Dancing in Soot   Name _____   Date _____

What do you think the family really thought
about the mess that Deirdre and David got into?

Mum

Dad

Aunt Dinah

Grandad

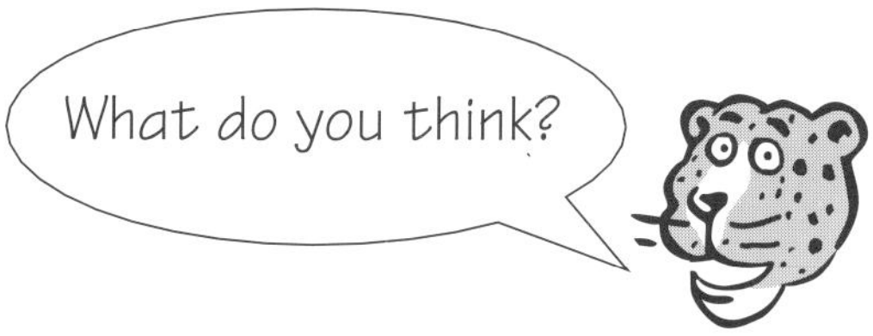

What do you think?

The Haystack

Author Richard Brown

Illustrator Susan Williams

Strand stories of childhood

Towards Independence: B

Other books in the strand at this stage

- A Welsh Lamb
- Dancing in Soot

Introducing the book

- Talk about the cover, including the title and blurb. Invite predictions about the book's contents.

- Explain that this is a true story that was told to the author by Joan Gallop, who was about eight when it happened in 1943 (her name was Joan Bailey then).

- Show the children some pictures of Britain at war in the 1940s to help them understand the story's setting and the references to the war.

After reading the book

- Discuss Brian's good and bad points, suggesting words to describe him.

- Discuss how Brian put himself in danger by not following basic safety rules.

WORKSHEET 1
Reading Development

Activity *Comprehension: true/false*

- Ask the children to read through the list of statements and to talk about each one.

- Check that they understand what 'true' and 'false' mean.

- Explain that they should write either 'true' or 'false' beside each statement. For some children it may be sufficient to mark 'T' or 'F'.

- They can check their answers by referring to the book and writing the page numbers in the boxes provided.

Answers 1 True, 2 False, 3 True, 4 False, 5 True, 6 False, 7 True, 8 False.

Extension activity

- The children could work in pairs and role-play the scene where the policeman questions Brian.

WORKSHEET 2
Personal Response

Activity *Writing a report*

- Refer to the picture on the worksheet. Ask the children as a group to say what happened to Brian, taking it in turns to tell the story.

- Ask the children whether they have ever had an accident themselves or have known anyone who had. They should share some of their stories. (You may find it useful to refer to the school's accident book for ideas.)

- The children can then fill in the accident report, using either their own story or one of those told by the others. They should draw the main character in the box on the right.

Extension activity

- The children could explain to a partner what the rescuer did.

The Haystack Name _____ Date _____

Read these statements.

Write **true** or *false* in the second column.

Write the page numbers in the third column.

	True or false	Page
1. The haystack was very big.		
2. We only ever caught one rat.		
3. The fire-fighters would not burn the haystack down because it might be needed.		
4. The mums were more worried about the height of the haystack than about the rats.		
5. Brian was knocked out when he fell off the haystack.		
6. Two boys had borrowed some matches.		
7. Brian lit his fire with a burning twig.		
8. Brian slept under the table.		

Worksheet 1 Reading Development

The Haystack   Name _____   Date _____

One day, Brian went too near the edge of the top of the haystack. All of a sudden, it gave way.

Have you ever had an accident?
Or do you know someone who has?
Fill in this accident report.

Name _____

Age _____

Date of accident _____

Where did it happen? _____

What happened?

Who came to the rescue? _____

176   Worksheet 2 Personal Response   © CUP 1996. Original artwork by Susan Williams.

A Shoot of Corn

Author Richard Brown

Illustrator Gillian Marklew

Strand stories of childhood

Towards Independence: C

Other books in the strand at this stage

- Snow in the Kitchen
- The Watch by the Sea

Introducing the book

- Talk about the cover, including the title and blurb. Invite predictions about the book's contents.

- Make sure that the children understand that this is a true story, as explained in the notes on the inside cover of the book. The events happened to the author, Richard Brown, in 1958.

After reading the book

- Ask the children to talk about anything they or their family have grown from seed. How did they look after their plants?

- Discuss Richard's feelings when he discovered that his shoot of corn had died. Why did Mrs Crabbe move the seed pot from his desk?

WORKSHEET 1
Reading Development

Activity *Cloze; sequencing*

- Ask the children to read through the sentences, predicting what each missing word might be.

Answers pushed, hurried, flopped, planted, watched, poked, straightened, lifted.

- Once the children have written in the missing words, see if they can spot the -ed pattern. (Some children could be given the -ed clue to help them complete the cloze.)

- Ask the children what the pictures on the worksheet show. They will need to match each sentence against the appropriate picture.

- Most children should match and sequence the sentences without referring to the text. Then they should use the text to check their answers.

WORKSHEET 2
Personal Response

Activity *Exploring a character's emotions*

- In response to the first incomplete sentence on the worksheet, ask the children to brainstorm ideas. Gather clues from the pictures in the book, drawing particular attention to the variety of expressions on Richard's face.

- Explain that the children could write more than one idea for each incomplete sentence.

Extension activity

- The children could look carefully at the pictures in the book and make a list of things in them which have changed since Richard was at school.

A Shoot of Corn

Name _____ Date _____

Fill in the missing words.
Cut out the pictures as a block and stick them on a piece of paper.
Then cut out the sentences and stick them in the right order
beside the pictures.

1.	One morning, I came in to find that a little green shoot had _____ up out of the soil. My last seed was growing.
2.	On the Monday morning, I _____ into class and looked up at the cupboard. My lovely shoot of corn had _____ over and shrivelled.
3.	I _____ the seed of corn deep in the soil in my jar. I _____ it every day. I wasn't sure if anything would happen.
4.	When my seedling reached about six inches in height, I was afraid that it might flop over. I _____ a pencil into the soil beside it.
5.	After a few days, the shoot had _____ up. It poked up proudly, a good inch tall.
6.	Then one day, Mrs Crabbe _____ the jar out of the inkwell and placed it on top of the tall cupboard by her desk.

A Shoot of Corn

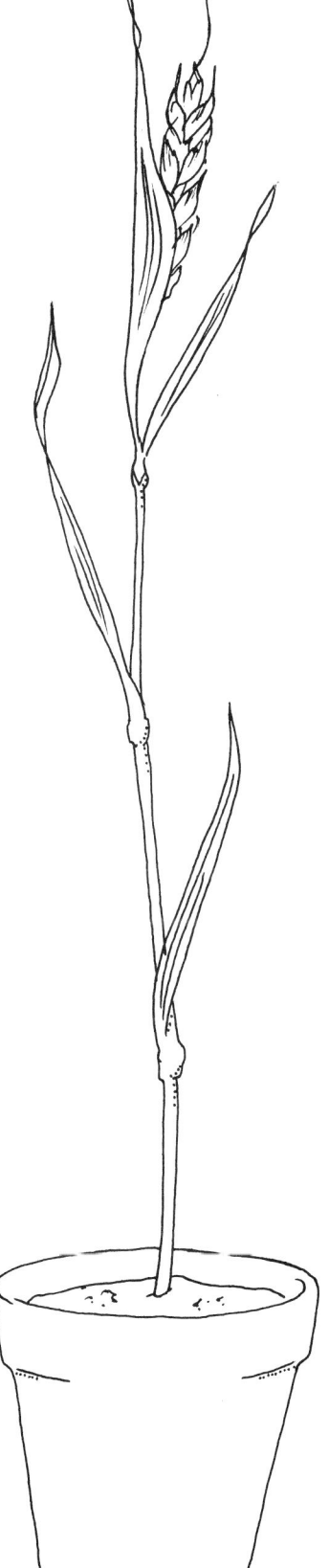

Complete these sentences.

I think the shoot of corn was very important to Richard because

When the shoot of corn was put on the tall cupboard, Richard should have asked for it back. He didn't because

If I ever plant a seed in a pot of soil, I shall make sure that

Snow in the Kitchen

Author Richard Brown

Illustrator Amanda Harvey

Strand stories of childhood

Towards Independence: C

Other books in the strand at this stage

- A Shoot of Corn
- The Watch by the Sea

Introducing the book

- Talk about the cover, including the title and blurb. Invite predictions about the book's contents.

- Explain that this is a true story told to the writer by Ciss Binns, who was remembering an event in her childhood in 1926. Show the photo of her on the inside of the back cover.

After reading the book

- Talk to the children about snow and what can be made from it.

- Ask the children why the miniature snow-scene was important to Ciss and why she remembered it for so long.

WORKSHEET 1
Reading Development

Activity *Cloze: vocabulary extension*

- The children should complete as much of the cloze as they can without referring to the book.

- When they have filled in as many blanks as they can, they should use the book to help them finish the worksheet. They will need to look at pages 2, 9, 11, 13, 16 and 17.

- All the children should check with the book to make sure their cloze is correct.

Answers *Left:* flakes, heavy, melting, sag, water.
Right: powdery, snowman, shower, drip.

WORKSHEET 2
Personal Response

Activity *Relating text to personal experience*

- Discuss Ciss's feelings as she made the snow-scene.

- Encourage the children to think about something they have made that they were proud of. Some of them can describe what they made.

- Ask the children to draw a picture showing what they made. Then they should complete the sentences about it.

- Before they begin, they could talk in pairs about what they are going to draw and write about.

Snow in the Kitchen   Name _____   Date _____

All these sentences, and parts of sentences, describe the snow.
Fill in the missing words.

Great _____

drifted down like feathers.

(page 2)

It was cool, _____

and light. (page 9)

The trees were

_____

with snow. (page 11)

The _____'s

head rolled off and broke

into a _____

of snow. (page 13)

"It's _____," I

cried, horrified to think that

all my work would soon slip

and _____ and

turn into puddles of

_____. (page 17)

The horses, the people and

the trees were beginning to

_____. (page 16)

Use a blue pencil to underline
the bits that are about
melting snow.

Worksheet 1 Reading Development   181

Ciss was very proud of her snow-scene.
Draw and write about something that you were proud of making.

I made it because

I made it out of

I was proud of it because

© CUP 1996. Original artwork by Amanda Harvey.

The Watch by the Sea

Author Richard Brown

Illustrator Annabel Large

Strand stories of childhood

Towards Independence: C

Other books in the strand at this stage

- A Shoot of Corn
- Snow in the Kitchen

Introducing the book

- Talk about the cover, including the title and blurb. Invite predictions about the book's contents.

- Explain that this is a story told to the writer by Brigit Andrews, who is remembering an event in her childhood in New Zealand in the 1950s. Show the photo on the inside back cover.

- Ask a child to point out where New Zealand is on a map.

After reading the book

- Re-read or retell the story, interspersing the narrative with questions about motives and feelings. For example: Why did Brigit disobey her mother and take the watch down to the beach? Was she brave or silly to go out on her own at night? Why didn't she tell anyone about the watch for years?

WORKSHEET 1
Reading Development

Activity *Exploring a character's emotions*

- Leaf through the book with the group, pausing at key points to ask how Brigit is feeling. Make a list of the words that the children use.

- The children can use the words on the list, as well as any others they have thought of themselves, to complete the worksheet.

- Ask the children to compare their answers.

WORKSHEET 2
Personal Response

Activity *Relating text to personal experience*

- Ask the children to tell you about what happened at a time when they once lost, or mislaid, something which was important to them.

- Encourage the children to use the worksheet to retell a true event, if possible. Alternatively, they could make up a story in which they lose something.

- Help them to organise their retelling by using the questions on the worksheet as a framework.

The Watch by the Sea Name _____ Date _____

How did Brigit feel during each part of the story?

	When she was given the watch, she felt	When she heard it ticking by her bed at night, she felt
When she played on the beach, she felt	When she took her watch down to the beach, she felt	When she looked for her watch under the bed, she felt
When she knew that she had lost the watch, she felt	When she climbed out of the window into the dark, she felt	When she walked towards the moonlit sea, she felt
When she ran home, she felt	When she stared at her bare wrist the next morning, she felt	

© CUP 1996. Original artwork by Annabel Large.

The Watch by the Sea

Name _____ Date _____

Write a story about losing something.
It can be true, or you can imagine it.

What did you lose?

Why was it important?

Where did you lose it?

> Once I had a

What did you do when you knew that it was lost?

How did you feel?

> When I knew that I'd lost my

What happened in the end?

What did you do?

> In the end,

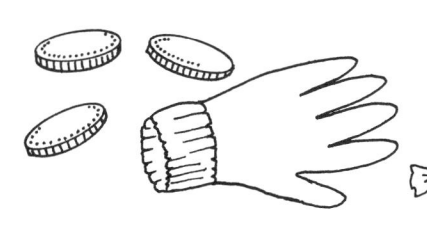

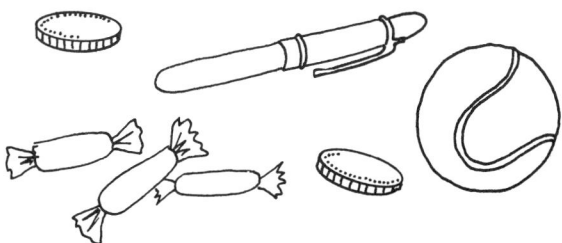

Worksheet 2 Personal Response   185

In the Mirror

Chosen by Richard Brown and Kate Ruttle

Illustrator Irene Trivas

Strand poetry

Towards Independence: A

Other books in the strand at this stage

- Marvel Paws
- Nonsense!

Introducing the book

- Talk about the cover, including the title and blurb. Invite predictions about the book's contents.
- If necessary, explain that these are all poems about 'me'.
- Let the children look quickly through the book, and then ask them why they think it has been called *In the Mirror*.

Using the book

- See the notes on pages 22–24.
- Read the poem 'The Leader' (page 17), first with expression and then without. Talk to the children about how the way we read affects the poem. Get them to read it to each other in pairs and to talk together about how it sounded.
- Read the poem 'The End' (page 10). Ask the children if they can add more verses to the poem, using the rhyme to help them.

WORKSHEET 1
Reading Development

Activity *Labelling*

- Ask a child to read or recite the poem 'Who Is It?' A second child could touch the body parts referred to.
- Before completing the worksheet, the children should think about whether there are any other labels they could put on, using a dictionary to help.

Extension activity

- The children could draw an amazing monster and label their drawings. Then ask them to rewrite the poem, putting in different numbers to describe the monster they have drawn (e.g. two heads, no shoulders, three knees and six toes).
- Put all the monsters into one big class book.

WORKSHEET 2
Personal Response

Activity *Drawing: wishes*

- Ask the children to read the poem 'Only the Lonely' (page 16).
- Discuss the pros and cons of having a room of your own and of sharing a room.
- Explain that the activity is about a room the children *would like to have*, whether they already have their own room or not.

Extension activity

- Make a Venn diagram with the children showing times when they would rather be alone and times when they would like to be with their friends or family.

Circle all the body part words.

Take...

A head, some shoulders, knees, and toes,

A mouth and eyes that see,

A pair of legs, two feet, one nose,

And what you've got is

ME!

Draw yourself here. Add labels.

Use the words in the poem to label your picture.

In the Mirror

Read 'Only the Lonely'.
Circle things that you would like to do in a room of your own.
Draw four things you would like to have in your room.

lie down

be alone

play with friends

watch TV

draw

play

sit

read

write

j u m p

think

talk

be quiet

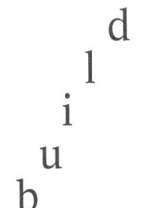

build

play with Lego

listen to tapes

s–l–e–e–p

Worksheet 2 Personal Response   © CUP 1996. Original artwork by Irene Trivas.

Marvel Paws

Chosen by Richard Brown
and Kate Ruttle

Illustrator David Parkins

Strand poetry

Other books in the strand at this stage

- In the Mirror
- Nonsense!

Introducing the book

- Talk about the cover, including the title and blurb. Invite predictions about the book's contents.
- If necessary, explain that these are all poems about pets.

Using the book

- See the notes on pages 22–24.
- Read the poem 'I Want . . .' (page 22) and discuss what it would be like to have a rat or frog for a pet.
- Ask each child to choose one poem that they would like to read. Some children could then read the one they chose to the others and say what they enjoyed about it.
- Ask the children to talk about pets that they have or would like. Discuss what makes an animal a pet.

WORKSHEET 1
Reading Development

Activity *Sequencing*

- Get the children to close their books and listen. Read through the poem 'Cats' (page 13) a couple of times and then again, leaving gaps for the children to fill in. Discuss with them how they are able to decide which words to put (rhyme, syntax and meaning).
- Ask the children to cut out the poem on the worksheet and sequence it without referring to the book.
- Discuss the illustrations the children need to do for each strip.
- The children should use the strips to make a small book (see page 32).

Extension activity

- The children could record their readings of the poem, and then together evaluate the recordings.

WORKSHEET 2
Personal Response

Activity *Classifying; ranking in order of preference*

- Ask the children to leaf through the book and say what animal each poem (except the last one) is about.
- Choose one of the animals and brainstorm words to describe it. Record the results as a word-web.
- Show the children how to complete the chart by filling it in for one animal. (If you would prefer to use a different set of attributes from those on the chart, white out the ones on the master copy and write in your own.)
- To stimulate discussion, the task could be done in pairs, using one worksheet for each pair.
- Before the children rank their own list of the pets, you could suggest they write the names of the pets on slips of paper and move the order of them around as they discuss them with a partner. They can then record the final order on the worksheet.

Parts of the poem are mixed up here.
Cut them out and put them in the right order.
Add drawings and make a strip book.

Any chair,
Top of piano,
Window-ledge,

Fitted in a
Cardboard box,

They don't care!
Cats sleep
Anywhere.

In the cupboard
With your frocks –
Anywhere!

Cats sleep
Anywhere,
Any table,

In the middle
On the edge,

Anybody's
Lap will do,

Open drawer,
Empty shoe,

Marvel Paws   Name_____   Date_____

Tick the words that describe each pet.

There are poems in the book about all these pets.

	cuddly	noisy	messy	lively
cat				
worm				
parakeet				
dog				
duck				
mice				
puppy				
goat				

Write a list of the pets here.
Start with the one that you like best.
Finish with the one that you like least.

1._____   5._____

2._____   6._____

3._____   7._____

4._____   8._____

Worksheet 2 Personal Response.   191

Nonsense!

Chosen by Richard Brown
and Kate Ruttle

Illustrator Martin Chatterton

Strand poetry

Other books in the strand at this stage

- In the Mirror
- Marvel Paws

Introducing the book

- Talk about the cover, including the title and blurb. Invite predictions about the book's contents.
- If necessary, explain that these are all nonsense poems.

Using the book

- See the notes on pages 22–24.
- Focus on the poem 'My Name Is . . .' (page 17). Ask the children to make up another verse together, based on similar nonsense.
- Encourage the children to read poems to each other. Discuss the importance of rhythm and pace in making each poem effective, and how the rhyme creates a musical quality.

WORKSHEET 1
Reading Development

Activity *Cloze; sequencing; matching*

- The children should compare the two rhymes 'Little Miss Muffet' and 'Little Miss Tucket' on pages 20 and 21.
- Ask the children to identify the words that are missing on the worksheet.

Answers

too	cream	scream
her	her	stew

Extension activity

- Look at other nursery rhymes with the children (e.g. 'Baa, Baa, Black Sheep', 'Hickory Dickory Dock', 'Twinkle, Twinkle', 'Old MacDonald'). Ask them to think about how they could change these.
- Put these into a book called *Nonsense Nursery Rhymes*. The children could read these to younger classes, or the rhymes could be taped for class members or other children to listen to.

WORKSHEET 2
Personal Response

Activities *Choosing favourite poems*

- Ask the children which poem they would choose if they could keep only one rhyme from this book. Get them to share their reasons.
- Some children will need line guides in the space provided for copying their favourite poem, enough for all the lines in the poem. They will need to use a separate piece of paper if they choose a long poem.
- If some children find copying difficult, photocopy their chosen poem for them so that they can stick it into the space.
- Once they have done the worksheet, ask some children to read out their favourite poem to the rest of the class. Encourage them all to learn at least one poem by heart – their favourite one, or a different one if they prefer.

Extension activity

- The children could make their own anthology of nonsense rhymes – group or individual – for handwriting practice or to develop word-processing skills. Make sure other nonsense rhyme collections are available for the children to dip into.

Nonsense!

Name _____ Date _____

Fill in the missing rhyming words.
Cut out the boxes and match them to the pictures and nursery rhymes. Draw
the last picture for each nursery rhyme yourself.

And so she ate him up _____ .	Little Miss Tucket Sat on a bucket Eating some peaches and _____ .	She said, "Go away or I'll _____!"
There came a big spider Who sat down beside _____ .	Along came a spider Who sat down beside _____ .	Little Miss Muffet Sat on a tuffet Eating her Irish _____ .

Nonsense!

Name _____   Date _____

Copy your favourite nonsense poem here.

Write the titles of three other poems that you like.
Say why you like them.

Title	Page	Why I like the poem

Worksheet 2 Personal Response

A Corner of Magic

Chosen by Richard Brown and Kate Ruttle

Illustrator Francesca Pelizzoli

Strand poetry

Towards Independence: B

Other books in the strand at this stage

- A Lick of the Spoon
- Knickerbocker Number Nine

Introducing the book

- Talk about the cover, including the title and blurb. Invite predictions about the book's contents.
- Explain that this is a collection of story poems.
- Discuss the children's choices and preferences of reading material. Do they choose poetry books? Why? Why not?

Using the book

- See the notes on pages 22–24.
- Read and discuss the first story poem, 'Forbidden Poem' (page 4). What do the children think it is about? Why does it say they might never be the same again? What might happen to them?
- Read through some of the poems, encouraging the children to join in. Then discuss which ones were the most popular.
- Read 'The Owl and the Pussy-Cat' (page 10) and 'Solomon Grundy' (page 18). Ask the children to explain why these are both story poems, even though they are of quite different lengths.

WORKSHEET 1
Reading Development

Activity *Cloze: vocabulary extension*

- Read 'This is the Key' (page 6) with the children, encouraging them to join in. It could be read or recited in a circle, each child taking one line, or all the children could call out the last word of each line as you come to it.
- The muddled-up part of the poem has most of the details in reverse order. Ask the children if they can spot what is wrong with it.
- Ask the children to fill in the blanks in the second version together, using the clue they have found and the picture clues. See how much of it they can remember and complete without looking at the book.

WORKSHEET 2
Personal Response

Activity *Extension of own ideas*

- For each suggestion on the worksheet, ask for the children's opinions for and against, backed up with accounts of what could have happened in each situation.
- Record other suggestions about why Humpty fell that emerge in the discussion.
- Before the children write their idea down, discuss the best way to start (e.g. 'I think Humpty fell because . . .', 'Perhaps he fell because . . .' or 'No-one knows the answer to this, but it may have happened like this: . . .').

Extension activity

- The children could develop their ideas into story-telling, telling each other the full story of Humpty's fall.

A Corner of Magic   Name _____   Date _____

Someone has muddled the first part of this poem up!

This is the key of the kingdom:
In that kingdom there are some flowers.
In those flowers there is a basket.
On that basket there is a bed.
In that bed there is a room.
In that room there is a house.
In that house there is a yard.
In that yard there is a lane.
In that lane there is a street.
In that street there is a town.
In that town there is a city.

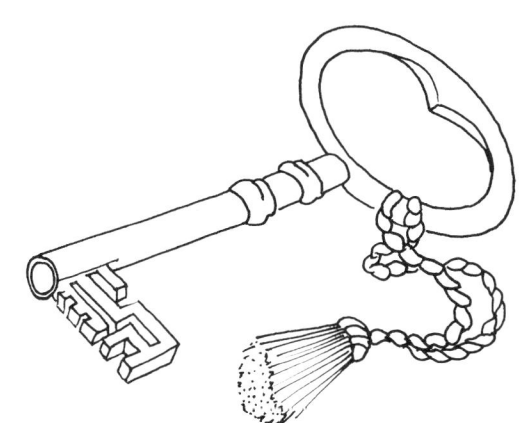

Write the lines correctly.

This is the key of the kingdom.

In that kingdom there is a city.

In that _____ there is a _____.

In that _____ there is a _____.

In that _____ there is a _____.

In that _____ there is a _____.

In that _____ there is a _____.

In that _____ there is a _____.

In that _____ there is a _____.

On that _____ there is a _____.

In that _____ there are some _____.

A Corner of Magic

Name _____ Date _____

Read 'Humpty' on page 15.

Why did Humpty fall off the wall?

No-one knows the answer to that.

Did he lose his balance?

Was he pushed?

Did he doze off?

Was he blown off?

Did he want to see if he could bounce?

Did all the king's men frighten him?

Talk about these ideas with a partner.
Then write down why you think Humpty fell off the wall.

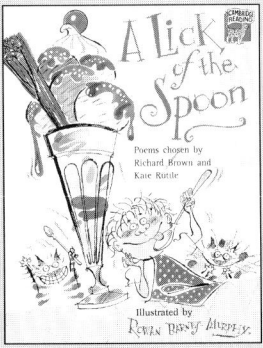

A Lick of the Spoon

Chosen by Richard Brown and Kate Ruttle

Illustrator Rowan Barnes-Murphy

Strand poetry

Towards Independence: B

Other books in the strand at this stage

• A Corner of Magic

• Knickerbocker Number Nine

Introducing the book

• Talk about the cover, including the title and blurb. Invite predictions about the book's contents.

• If necessary, explain that all the poems are about food.

• Look at the contents page with the children. See if it is possible for them to predict what foods some of the poems are about.

Using the book

• See the notes on pages 22–24.

• Read the poem 'The Hardest Thing to Do in the World' (page 8) and discuss any similar experiences the children might have had. Discuss the fact that not all poems rhyme.

• Focus on the poems 'Phew!' (page 9) and 'After All the Digging' (page 21). Discuss the way the poems have been arranged on the page.

WORKSHEET 1
Reading Development

Activity *Finding information; using quotations*

• Ask the children to read the worksheet. Check if they are able to remember or find out what foods the words are referring to.

Answers *Left:* swedes, gum, lolly. *Right:* coconut, cabbage, pancake.

• The children should then find two more quotations from the book and copy them out in the space provided, adding the page numbers. They could draw bubbles round them like the ones on the worksheet.

Extension activity

• The children could write their own descriptions of or poems about their favourite foods, combining them to make a class book.

WORKSHEET 2
Personal Response

Activity *Writing a poem*

• Read the poem 'My Sweet' (page 17) with the children.

• Draw their attention to the sequence described by the first line of verses 2, 3 and 4.

• Ask the children to suggest feelings and tastes that might be associated with a sweet that they would invent.

• Create a list of descriptive phrases suggested by the children.

• Point out that the original poem is not written in rhyme, and that their poem does not have to rhyme.

Extension activity

• The children could design an advertisement for their new sweet.

A Lick of the Spoon

Name _____ Date _____

Which foods are these poems describing?

crisp, crunchy
(page 23)

like a football in
the sky (page 22)

chomp, chomp,
slurp, chomp
(page 15)

dead green
(page 12)

lovely, juicy, ice-cold,
mouth-watering,
tongue-numbing,
melting (page 9)

mix it,
stir it,
fry it,
toss it (page 4)

Copy your own favourite lines.

A Lick of the Spoon   Name _____   Date _____

Read the poem 'My Sweet'.
Invent your own sweet to finish off this poem.

Draw your sweet here.

Shall I tell you about the sweet

I'm going to invent?

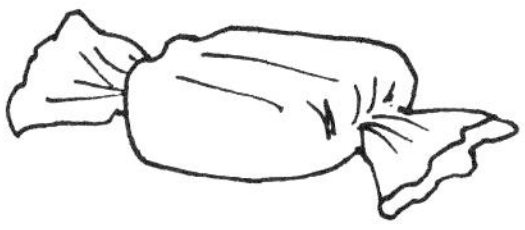

When you first pop it in

_____

_____

_____

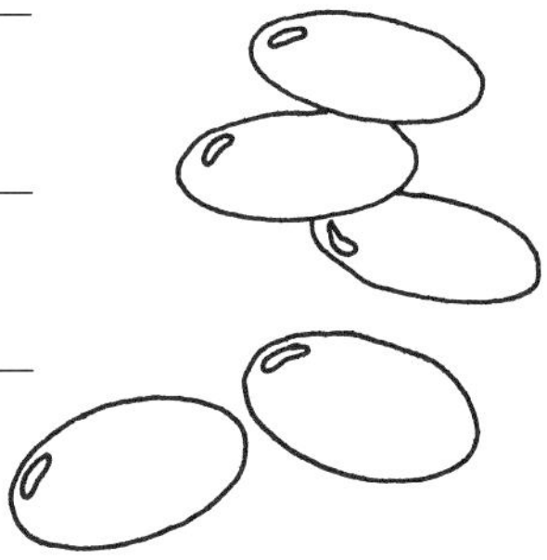

And when you start to chew

_____

_____

And when you swallow my sweet

_____

_____

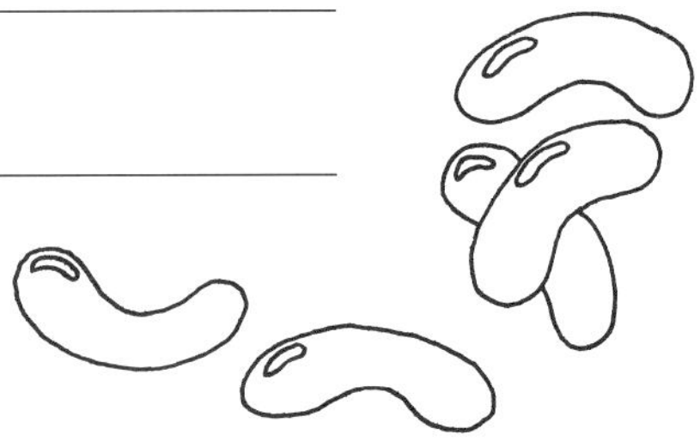

Would you like one?

Knickerbocker Number Nine

Chosen by Richard Brown
and Kate Ruttle

Illustrators John Bendall-Brunello
and Sarah McDonald

Strand poetry

Towards Independence: B

Other books in the strand at this stage

- A Corner of Magic
- A Lick of the Spoon

Introducing the book

- Talk about the cover, including the title and blurb. Invite predictions about the book's contents.

- If necessary, explain that all the poems are about games and pastimes.

Using the book

- See the notes on pages 22–24.

- Ask the children to look through the contents page and choose a poem to read that they think sounds interesting. Let them read it silently to themselves, then ask them if they would like to read it to the others. Encourage the children to comment on it.

- Discuss whether the title of a poem gives enough information to judge what it is about.

- Focus on the very active poem 'Doctor Knickerbocker', and discuss rhythm and pace. Let the children listen to and watch each other reading it. Can they speed up and slow down?

WORKSHEET 1
Reading Development

Activity *Rhyming cloze; sequencing*

- Ask the children to find the poem that starts with the line 'Five silver jacks'. If necessary, remind them that the index of first lines will help them. Read the poem through with them and then close the book before moving on to the worksheet.

- Make sure the children refer to the rhyming pattern in each verse when filling in the missing words.

- Ask the children to cut out the nine boxes and order the verses of the poem without looking at the book. When they have ordered the poem to their satisfaction, they should check their solution by referring back to the book.

Extension activity

- Discuss what games the children play outside or at parties (e.g. musical chairs, chase, pass the parcel). Ask them to describe the rules of one of these games.

WORKSHEET 2
Personal Response

Activity *Writing a poem*

- Ask the children to find and read the poem 'Wings'.

- See if the children can name their five senses. Ask them to read the second line in each verse and identify which of the senses is being used. Point out that the sixth verse is not about one of the five senses.

- Before they write their own poem, they will need to think of things that they can find out through using each of their senses.

- Make sure the children understand that their poem should be about the possibilities that would be created if they had wings.

Extension activity

- The children could make a class book entitled 'If I had . . .' Suggest that they write poems about having fins, tails, paws and so on.

This poem is about the game of Jacks.
Write in the missing rhyming words.
Cut out the verses and put them in the right order.

Five silver jacks,
All in a row...
Here, take the ball –
Would you like a

_____ ?

Five silver jacks.
One rubber ball,
A playground game
For one and _____ .

Throw the ball,
Here I go,
I'll try for five –
Can I?   _____ !

Throw the ball,
Pick up one,
Now our game
Has just _____ .

Throw the ball...
Pick up...four!
Whoops! I've
  dropped
One on the _____ .

Throw the ball,
Pick up... three!
One for you
And two for

_____ .

Throw the ball,
Try again...
I've got all five!
I could do _____ !

Throw the ball,
Pick up two,
One for me
And one for

_____ .

Knickerbocker Number Nine   Name _____

Read the poem 'Wings'.
What would you do if you had wings? Write your own poem in the spaces.

 If I had wings

I would touch _____

and _____ .

 If I had wings

I would taste _____

and _____ .

 If I had wings

I would listen to _____

and _____ .

 If I had wings

I would gaze at _____

and _____ .

If I had wings

I would smell _____

and _____ .

Worksheet 2 Personal Response   203

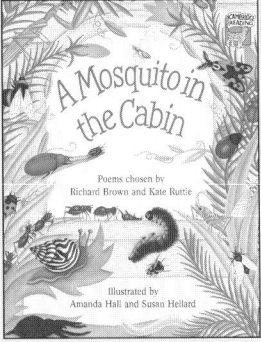

A Mosquito in the Cabin

Chosen by Richard Brown and Kate Ruttle

Illustrators Amanda Hall and Susan Hellard

Strand poetry

Towards Independence: C

Other books in the strand at this stage

- Out and About
- Welcome Night

Introducing the book

- Talk about the cover, including the title and blurb. Invite predictions about the book's contents.
- If necessary, explain that all these poems are about minibeasts.
- Look at the index of first lines and see if the children are able to guess what kind of minibeast each poem might be about.

Using the book

- See the notes on pages 22–24.
- Let the children read silently through the poems on their own and select a poem that they would like to read to the others or a friend. Encourage them to explain why they liked the poem they chose.
- Read the final poem, 'Hurt No Living Thing'. Ask the children what they think about the message of the poem.

After reading the book

- Discuss what the best uses of the index of first lines might be.

WORKSHEET 1
Reading Development

Activity *Alliteration*

- Explain to the children that alliteration occurs when several words close together begin with the same sound.
- Ask the children to think of an alliterative adjective to go with their own name (e.g. Careful Kate, Happy Hardip, Funny Philip). Make sure that the children understand that alliteration relates to sound, not spelling.
- When the children have identified the alliterative sounds given on the worksheet, ask them to hunt through the book to find more examples. They will learn most from this activity if they work co-operatively in pairs, or perhaps small groups.

WORKSHEET 2
Personal Response

Activity *Extension of ideas: tabulating*

- The children should use the contents page to find each of the minibeasts listed.
- The poems contain some ideas about how to handle the different minibeasts. The children should use these to complete the worksheet, and then use their own ideas and experiences to add more ticks to the list.
- When the children have completed their lists, they should compare them and discuss any discrepancies.

A Mosquito in the Cabin   Name _____

Sometimes in poetry you will find words close together which begin with the same sound. This is called 'alliteration'.

Circle the words in these lines that have alliterative sounds.

Busy buzzer, busy bee   ('Bee')

The speckled air of summer stars   ('Fireflies')

...the damp dewdrops fall   ('Ladybird! Ladybird!')

Phew! It's flying off again!   ('The Fly')

Look through the book and find some more lines with alliteration in them. Write them here.

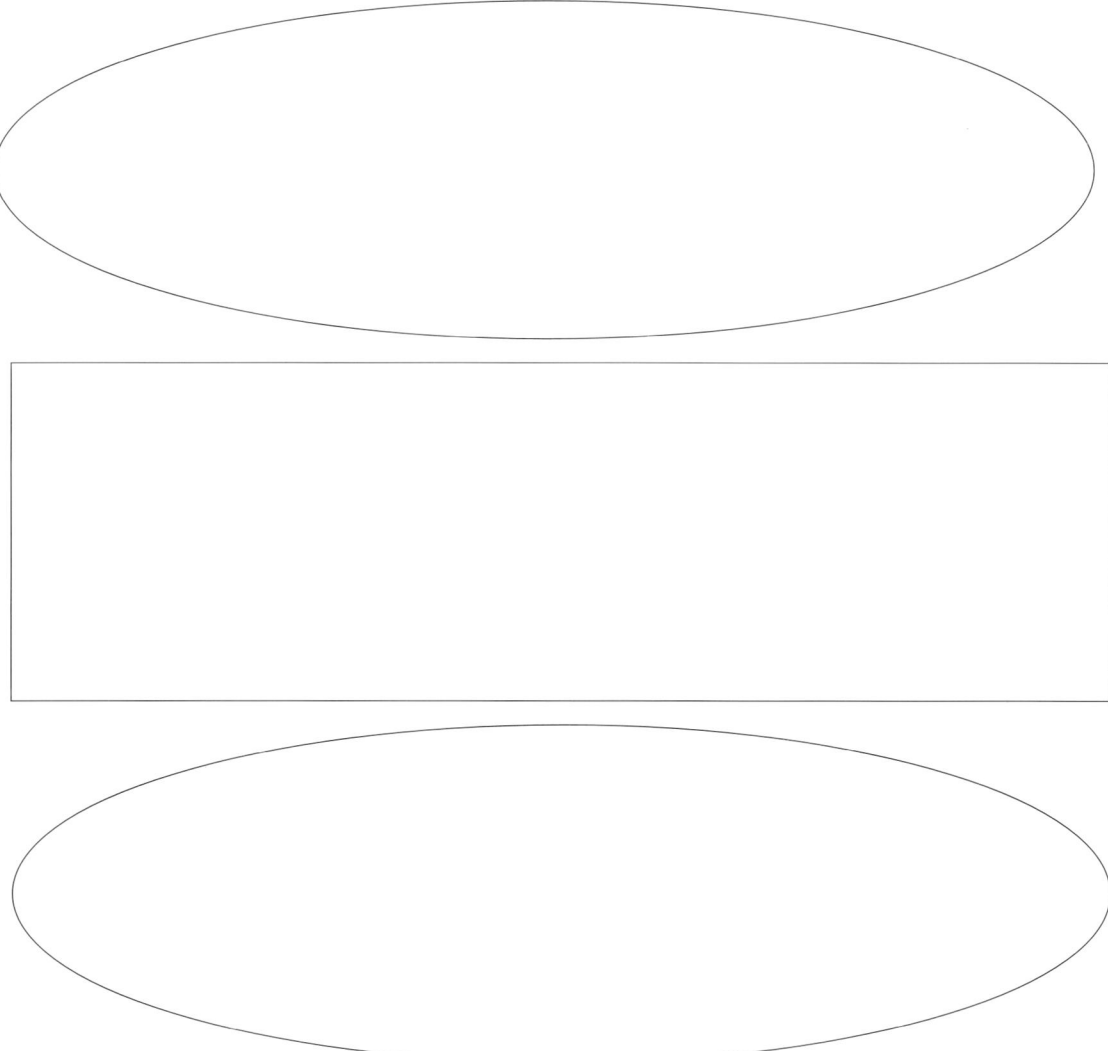

A Mosquito in the Cabin

Name _____

Read the poems carefully. Look for ideas about how to handle minibeasts.

Which suggestions are a good idea for each of these minibeasts?
Tick all the boxes that you think are right.

Minibeast	Hold it	Swat it	Watch it	Run from it	Let it go
Snail					
Caterpillar					
Fly					
Spider					
Moth					
Earthworm					
Mosquito					
Dragonfly					
Ladybird					

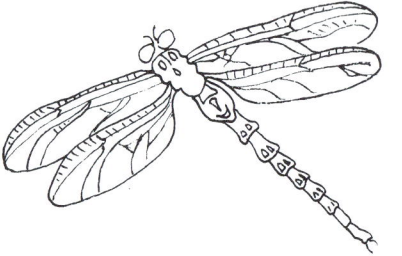

Discuss your list with a friend.

Out and About

Chosen by Richard Brown
and Kate Ruttle

Illustrators Amanda Harvey
and Lisa Kopper

Strand poetry

Towards Independence: C

Other books in the strand at this stage

• A Mosquito in the Cabin

• Welcome Night

Introducing the book

• Talk about the cover, including the title and blurb. Invite predictions about the book's contents.

• If necessary, explain that all these poems are about the outside world.

• Look at the index of first lines and see if the children are able to guess what some of the poems might be about.

Using the book

• See the notes on pages 22–24.

• Read the poem 'Change' (page 28). Discuss the times of the year that the children prefer. Ask them whether they like the differences they notice about the seasons. Why? Why not?

• Ask the children to read through the poems and to choose two that are about two different times of the year. They should share these with a partner by reading and listening.

• Look together at the poem 'Until I Saw the Sea' (page 10). Discuss whether the descriptions of the sea are good ones.

WORKSHEET 1
Reading Development

Activity *Sequencing using rhyme*

• Discuss with the children the rhythm of the poem 'White Fields' (page 26) and its rhyming pattern.

• Ask the children to rearrange the jumbled lines so that the poem makes sense. Discuss what strategies or clues they might use to help them.

• If necessary, remind them that they can use the contents page to find the poem.

WORKSHEET 2
Personal Response

Activity *Relating a poem to personal experience*

• Discuss different ideas about what an adventure might be.

• Make a list with the children of all the different places and possibilities suggested in the poems where adventures might happen.

• Ask the children to suggest more kinds of adventures and add them to the list.

• Encourage the children to read and answer the questions on the worksheet before they begin to write.

Cut out the poem and match the two-line verses.
Put the pieces in the right order.

Walking in the fields of snow;

Where there is no grass at all;

Is as white as white can be

Pointing out the way we came –

Prints in silver filigree;

And our mothers always know,

White Fields

In winter-time we go

Where the top of every wall,

Every fence, and every tree,

Every one of them the same –

All across the fields there be

By the footprints in the snow,

Where it is the children go.

Name _____ Date _____

Read 'Morning Song'.

What kind of adventure would you like to have?

Where would you go?

How would you get there?

Who would you go with?

What would you take with you?

What would you do when you got there?

Welcome Night

Chosen by Richard Brown
and Kate Ruttle

Illustrator Nick Maland

Strand poetry

Towards Independence: C

Other books in the strand at this stage

- A Mosquito in the Cabin

- Out and About

Introducing the book

- Talk about the cover, including the title and blurb. Invite predictions about the book's contents.

- If necessary, explain that all these poems are about night.

Sharing the book

- See the notes on pages 22–24.

- Select a poem that you enjoy. Read this with the children and tell them what you liked about it. This gives you an opportunity to model for them how to explain, explore, reason and describe preferences.

- Alternatively, start with the first poem, which looks at night from a child's experience. Talk to the children about what this makes them feel about night and explore their feelings regarding night and darkness.

- Ask the children to read the poems aloud as a group or silently to themselves. They may then select one that they want to read with a partner and discuss their choice.

- Focus on the poem 'Night Street' (page 16). Ask three children to take the three parts of the poem. The rest of the group should join in by reading the italic text. Explore the feelings of the child in bed. Ask the children what words or phrases create a scary feeling.

WORKSHEET 1
Reading Development

Activity *Sentence completion; vocabulary extension*

- Ask the children to go through the book and note which poems in particular refer to the moon. Discuss the phrases and adjectives used to describe the moon.

- The children should try to fill in the missing words without referring to the book. Then ask them to use the page numbers to check their answers.

- To create the moon word-web the children can use descriptions in the poems or their own words.

Extension activity

- The children could use the words on their moon word-web to write their own poem or description.

WORKSHEET 2
Personal Response

Activity *Relating poems to personal experience*

- Talk to the children about night fears, discussing why some sights and sounds which are not worrying in the light can appear threatening at night.

- Ask the children to read 'I Like to Stay Up' and 'Night Street'. Remind them that they can use the contents page to find them.

- Discuss what frightens the children in these poems.

- Make a list of things which are frightening in the light, and a separate list of things which are frightening in the dark.

- Use the lists to remind the children how to complete a Carroll diagram.

Welcome Night   Name _____   Date _____

Many of the poems in this book describe the moon.
Complete these descriptions.

Moon comes

_____,

_____.

(page 8)

The Moon is

her

_____,

(page 9)

In the
ocean of the sky
Through a wave-rising
of clouds

_____

_____

(page 10)

The

moon was a

_____

_____

tossed upon
cloudy seas,

(page 29)

Make a word-web of words
describing the moon.

Welcome Night

Name _____ Date _____

Write these words and phrases in the diagram to show what frightens you. You can write each word or phrase in more than one box.

being alone

being awake   dreaming

moving shadows

footsteps outside   giants, dragons,

goblins   storms   owl calls

odd, creaky noises

	frightens me	does not frighten me
in the dark		
in the light		

Write one more thing in each box of the diagram.

212   Worksheet 2 Personal Response   © CUP 1996. Original artwork by Nick Maland.